SCHOLASTIC

Year 1
Scottish Primary 2

50 Shared texts

INCLUDES CD-ROM

NON-FICTION

Claire Head and David Waugh

Credits

Authors
David Waugh and
Claire Head

Series Consultants
Huw Thomas
Melissa Mackinlay

Project Manager
Elizabeth Dalby

Editor
Roanne Charles

Assistant Editor
Rachel Mackinnon

Series Designer
Anna Oliwa

Designers
Lynne Joesbury
Helen Taylor
Micky Pledge

Text © 2007 David Waugh and Claire Head
© 2007 Scholastic Ltd

Designed using Adobe InDesign

Published by Scholastic Ltd
Villiers House
Clarendon Avenue
Leamington Spa
Warwickshire CV32 5PR

www.scholastic.co.uk

Printed by Bell and Bain Ltd, Glasgow

1 2 3 4 5 6 7 8 9   7 8 9 0 1 2 3 4 5 6

British Library Cataloguing-in-Publication Data
A catalogue record for this book is available from the British Library.

ISBN 0-439-96564-0
ISBN 978-0439-96564-4

System requirements
- Supported PC operating systems: Windows 98 SE, Windows ME, Windows 2000, Windows NT, Windows XP
- Supported Mac operating systems: Mac OS9 with CarbonLib 1.6[1], Mac OSX
- Recommended minimum processor speed: 1GHz
- Recommended minimum RAM: 512MB

Mac OSX version 10.1 and Intel-based Macs
If you are experiencing problems, please double click the icon named "os9 autorun" on the CD-ROM. This will run the Mac OS9 version of the program.

[1]Some versions of Mac OS9 do not have CarbonLib 1.6 installed. Please visit the Apple website (www.apple.com) to download and install CarbonLib 1.6.

Contents

N *Teachers' notes*   **P** *Photocopiable*

Term 2

Term 3

N *Teacher's notes*   P *Photocopiable*

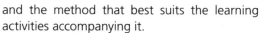

Introduction

The new *50 Shared Texts Non-fiction* series follows Scholastic's previously published series, *50 Shared Texts*. It picks up on two comments received from a number of teachers in response to the initial series. Firstly they welcomed the notes that accompanied each text, providing various avenues for discussion with a class as part of the shared or guided reading of the text. Secondly, they wanted more non-fiction. By 'more' they meant both 'more texts' in general, and texts from a wider range of backgrounds.

This new series aims to meet those needs, by building on the most valuable aspects of the original series. The provision of a range of high-quality extracts gives you the time to focus on teaching rather than sourcing material; relevant links with other areas of the curriculum are highlighted; and the book can be easily used in a flexible way and dipped into as required.

Shared reading

Shared reading has been around as a specific term since the work of Don Holdaway in New Zealand. The idea gained momentum during the 1980s but the main push for both 'shared' and 'guided' approaches to reading took off with the arrival of the National Literacy Strategy, introduced by the Government to schools in England and Wales in 1997. The approaches have also found a home in classrooms in Scotland and further afield.

Shared reading is the strategy in which the teacher reads a text with the whole class. This can be everyone reading along together or the teacher giving instructions such as 'read the first paragraph in your head'. It can include the teacher reading and pointing to the words while the children observe, or the teacher asking a child to read a portion of the text aloud. The key ingredient is everyone having sight of the same text and taking their eyes along the same lines at the same time.

This series incorporates a range of approaches to shared reading, dependent on the age of the children, the best approach to the specific text and the method that best suits the learning activities accompanying it.

While the series is entitled 50 Shared Texts it also allows for the fact that some teachers may want to use certain texts in the context of guided reading. Guided reading involves a teacher or teaching assistant working with a small group of children to guide them through a text, setting them off on their reading to a particular point, stopping them along the way and asking questions or discussing observations. The texts and notes in this resource can be used in this context.

What's in the book

The texts in this book are organised term by term, and cover a range of examples of non-fiction tailored to each year group. Each text appears in two forms. The small, annotated version and accompanying page of teachers' notes guide you through features in the text that lend themselves to learning objectives. The larger, un-annotated version is to use with your class and can be copied or enlarged.

What's on the CD-ROM

All 50 texts from the book also feature on the CD-ROM, in a variety of full-colour formats designed to maximise their potential for sharing with a group.

The CD-ROM contains:

● Colour versions of all 50 core texts.

● Fully annotated versions of the 50 core texts.

● Half-annotated versions of the 50 core texts, designed for use with interactive whiteboard tools – providing you with the opportunity to highlight, circle and underline key words and phrases.

● The 50 core texts in an editable format, allowing you or the children to make changes to the document and print out the results.

● Differentiated full-colour versions of all 50 texts. These are designed to support less able learners, though most can also be used with the whole class: to teach the structure of the various non-fiction genres, to scaffold writing tasks, or alongside the core text as a comparison between written and visual methods of presenting information.

● Print options for all the text versions.

The texts

The 50 core texts featured in the book and on the CD-ROM have been either gathered from a range of diverse backgrounds or specially written for this resource to fit with the objectives for each term. The crucial aim of this gathering is that it should save you time, providing you with a ready-to-use range of stimulating and appropriate magazine articles, website extracts, newspaper cuttings, reference material, advertisements, posters and leaflets to explore, rather than expecting you to spend time hunting them down yourself. For most text types, there is more than one example, allowing you to select the one that best supports your planning requirements.

The purpose-written texts have been devised to provide texts that dovetail with the objectives being explored in a particular unit of learning. The authors have aimed to cover a range of learning objectives, making full use of the texts to support text level objectives while also ensuring there is coverage at sentence and word level.

Background

Notes are provided about the text that may include details about its origin or author, the story behind it or the context in which it was printed. This section can also include notes from the author about the rationale for using a particular text in the way it is dealt with in this resource.

Discussing the text

Guidance is provided as to how each text can be explored in the classroom setting. The aim is to avoid bland questions and answers and to provide ways of engaging children in reading and interpreting the text. This can include discussion points, activities they may undertake that weave their way through a reading of the text, points of contention where they may disagree with it and language features that will lead them to further explore their own grasp of words.

Some of these sections contain a lot of material and it is up to you to be selective. The aim in each section is to provide more material than needed.

The texts

The choice of texts has been driven by the need to ensure that these are quality texts both in content and language. It is hoped that among the selection you will find a mixture of authors and texts, both familiar and new. Whole texts have been provided as far as possible so that children have the satisfaction of reading and appreciating a coherent and complete piece of writing.

Talk, read and write

This section leads on from the reading to provide activities stemming from the text. Following a discussion of the text, this section provides activities that link with the reading. These may lend themselves to independent or group work within literacy lessons or they could be activities that will fit in with other areas of the curriculum.

Extension

This section provides ideas for further exploration of themes covered in the text, and relevant homework activities suitable for the year group.

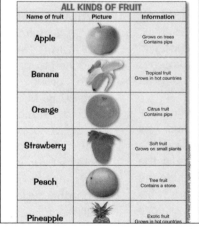

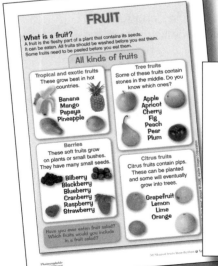

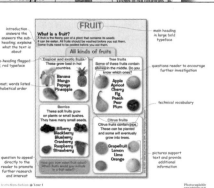

Range and objectives

Year 1 Term 1		
Range	**Text**	**NLS references**
Signs, labels, captions	**'Signs giving orders'** from the Department of Transport	W10, W12, T12, T14
	'School signs' by David Waugh	W10, T12, T14, T16
	'Walkers' map' by Claire Head	W10, T12, T13
	'Fantastic offers on garden tools!' by David Waugh	W10, W12, S3, S8, T12, T14
	'Leaves' from *Plants (Fascinating Science Series)* by Sally Hewitt	W4, W5, S4, T12, T13, T14
	'Flowering plants' by Claire Head	W12, S5, S6, S7, T16
	'Christmas in Europe' by David Waugh	S8, S9, T12, T14
	'How do we move?' from *Find out about the body* by Anita Ganeri	W12, S4, S8, S9, T14
	'Clothes' by Claire Head	W10, S4, T14, T15
Lists	**'Fruit'** by Claire Head	W10, S4, T1, T15
	'My food diary' by Claire Head	W8, W12, T14, T15
	'Shopping list' by David Waugh	W10, W12, T13, T15
	'School dinner menu' by Scholastic Ltd	W12, T2, T15
Instructional texts	**'Recipe: fruit salad'** by Claire Head	W8, T13, T14, T15
	'Light for life' from *Science for Fun: Light and Colour* by Gary Gibson	W12, S5, S6, T13, T15, T16
	'Plants and seeds – harvesting' from *Autumn* by Susan Humphries	W10, W12, S7, T12, T14
	'How to create an autumn leaves display' by Claire Head	W8, S4, T13, T14, T16

Year 1 Term 2

Range	Text	NLS references
Information books, including non-chronological reports	**'Model toys'** by Scholastic Ltd	W3, S7, T17, T24
	'Toys then and now' by David Waugh	W7, W10, T22, T23
	'My beautiful doll' by Scholastic Ltd	S7, T22, T23, T25
	'Touch' from *The Senses – Touch* edited by Mandy Suhr	W3, W7, T17, T25
	'Waste' from *Exploring where you live* by Terry Jennings	W4, W5, W10, T22, T23
	'A–Z' from *The A–Z of ghosts, skeletons and other haunting horrors* by Tracey Turner	W10, T17, T19
	'Index' from *Get Set Go! Vegetables* by Judy Bastyra	W3, W8, T21
	'How does a flower grow?' by Scholastic Ltd	W3, T17, T21
	'Contents and index' by Scholastic Ltd	W1, W8, T21, T24
	'Different kinds of homes' by Melissa Mackinlay	W10, S5, T20, T25
	'Houses and homes' by Melissa Mackinlay	W10, T17, T24, T25
Information books, including non-chronological reports, simple dictionaries	**'Squirrels'** by Claire Head	T17, T22, T24, T25
Information books, including non-chronological reports	**'Kittens'** by David Waugh	W3, S5, T17, T22, T25
	'The playground' by David Waugh	W3, S6, T23, T24
	'Playground fun' from www.playgroundfun.org.uk	S7, T22, T24
	'Looking after animals' from www.connexions-direct.com	W10, S6, T24, T25

Year 1 Term 3

Range	Text	NLS references
Information texts	**'Stay safe in the Sun'** by Claire Head	W6, W8, S5, T21
	'Make a string telephone' by Scholastic Ltd	S4, T17, T21
	'Why parks attract wildlife' from *Use your eyes: in the Park* by Ralph Whitlock	W1, W6, W8, S7, T19, T22
	'Garden birds' by David Waugh	W1, W7, S7, T17, T19, T22
	'House sparrows' by David Waugh	W1, S6, T17, T21
Information texts including recounts	**'The day I brought my first pet home'** by Claire Head	W2, S7, T18, T19, T21
	'Who cooks my school dinner?' by Claire Head	S5, T18, T19, T20
	'Diary of a PDSA vet' from secure.pdsa.org.uk/youngpdsa by Steve Howard	S5, T18, T19, T20
	'Trip to the park' illustrated by Simon Rumble	W8, S6, T18, T20
	'Kylie's life' by David Waugh	S5, T17, T18, T20, T21
	'Making toast' by David Waugh	W7, S6, T17, T21
	'A school trip to the seaside' by David Waugh	W1, S6, T18, T20
Information texts	**'KWL grid: Owls'** by Claire Head	W8, S7, T17, T22
Information texts: non-chronological reports	**'Owls'** by Claire Head	W8, S7, T19, T21, T22
	'Wrapping it up' from *How things are made* by Steve Parker	W9, S6, S7, T19, T22
	'What is a bike made of?' from *How things are made* by Steve Parker	W8, S7, T19, T21, T22
Information texts including recounts	**'Dear Tom'** by Claire Head	W1, W8, S5, T19

Signs giving orders

from the Department of Transport

Background

Children will be familiar with many of the road signs presented here, and should enjoy investigating the link between the shape and design of the signs and the information they give. The text should stimulate children to want to find signs in their environment and to discuss these at home. The text can be useful for helping children who have English as an additional language. In which case, it is worth investigating road signs in those children's countries to look for similarities and differences which can be discussed with everyone. This text can be linked to others which focus on labels and captions, in particular 'School signs', on page 12.

What's on the CD-ROM

The text on the CD-ROM has eight different signs with brief captions. They still consist of orders and warnings, however they are signs which the children are more likely to have seen in their day-to-day lives.

Discussing the text

● Begin by identifying signs which the children can see in the classroom and in the school, for example labels for particular areas of the room such as the book corner, fire exits, arrows pointing to offices, signs on toilet doors and office and classroom doors.

● Discuss how pictures and symbols are often used instead of words and ask the children why this is. Elicit that signs give important information. Pictures and symbols can be more easily understood by small children or by people who don't speak the language of the country they are visiting. They are also quicker to 'read' than lots of words.

● Talk about the signs which the children have seen on their way to school or near their homes. (You may need to warn the children in advance that they will be asked about this and tell them to look out for signs and talk to parents and carers about these.)

● Cover the captions and look at the signs on the text and talk about the differences between those signs which give orders and those which give warnings. For example, compare the warning triangle with a bicycle in the middle, which means *Warning – cycle route ahead*, and

the circular sign with a bicycle, which means *No cycling*. Make sure that the children understand the meanings of the words *circular* and *triangular* and the difference between a warning and an order.

● Ask the children to use the images to predict what the signs might mean. Then reveal and read the captions to check the predictions.

● Explain the warning sign for a level crossing without barriers which has a picture of a steam engine on it. Children may be interested to find out how long it is since steam trains were regularly seen on our railways!

Talk, read and write

● Look at the differentiated text from the CD-ROM and ask the children to point out the new signs. What do they think they mean? Do they warn or give orders?

● Ask the children to suggest other warnings or orders that might be useful for pedestrians or motorists. Try writing some captions to go with their ideas (for example, *water ahead* or *bumpy road*). Then ask the children to read these and design appropriate signs. Remind the children about the differences in shape of warning signs and those which give orders and ask them to tell you which shape each should be. Have a copy of the Highway Code available so that children can see if the signs they design match those which appear there.

● Practise spelling the key words, such as *bicycle, caravan, crossing* and *aircraft* and draw on the children's growing understanding of sound–symbol relationships to help them to build words.

Extension

Give children copies of the Highway Code or access to www.highwaycode.gov.uk and ask them to find signs for different road situations.

Ask children to draw and label different signs outside school, to make a display. Encourage them to look out for unusual and interesting signs such as warnings about deer, ducks and even frogs.

1: 1: T12: to read and use captions, such as labels around the school, on equipment

1: 1: T14: to write captions for their own work, such as for display, in class books

SIGNS GIVING ORDERS
No motor vehicles
No cycling
No towed caravans
STOP
Stop and give way
STOP
School crossing patrol
WARNING SIGNS
Patrol
School crossing patrol ahead
Pedestrian crossing
Cycle route ahead
Level crossing without barrier or gate ahead
Low flying aircraft or sudden aircraft noise
Cattle

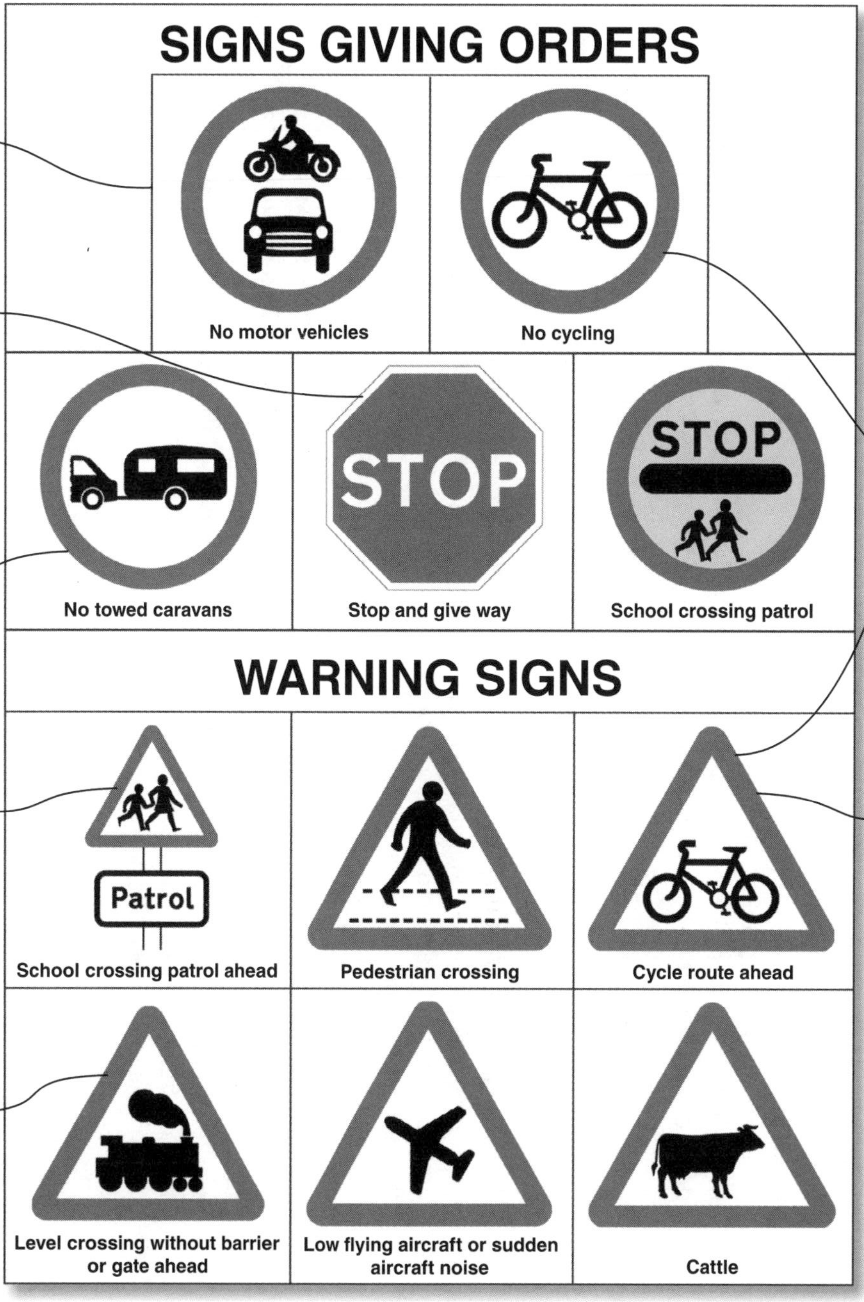

round signs = signs giving orders

has a word instead of an image

use of colour is important; red and black stand out clearly

has word plus image

image of steam train used; sign designed in early 20th century

very similar; only difference is shape of the sign

triangular signs = warning signs

1: 1: W12: to learn new words from reading and shared experiences, and to make collections of personal interest or significant words and words linked to particular topics

1: 1: W10: to recognise the critical features of words, such as length, common spelling patterns and words within words

School signs

by David Waugh

Background

Learning to decode and understand common signs is an important step to becoming a confident and independent member of the school community. This text comprises pictures of parts of a school and commonly found signs and labels. This text can be linked to others, including 'Signs giving orders' on page 10 and 'Plants and seeds – harvesting' on page 40, which feature captions. It can also be linked to geography work on patterns and processes. Many schools which have children from different countries with different first languages label things in these languages as well as in English. This activity could offer an opportunity to draw attention to these labels and to discuss the reasons for using them.

What's on the CD-ROM

This text shows the same contextual pictures, but the signs and labels are omitted to reduce the reading demands. As well as supporting whole-class discussion about the positioning of signs, this version can be annotated by children.

Discussing the text

● Before reading the text, ask the children to tell each other and then you what a label or sign is. Point to labels and signs in the classroom. Ask why people put labels on things. For example, drawers and cupboards may be labelled to show what they contain; children's clothes are often labelled with their names so that they can be returned if lost.

● Ask pairs to discuss some of the places around the school where labels and signs are seen, and then to share their thoughts with the class. Make a list of their ideas on the board. Pick out some of the suggested words and talk with the children about how they are spelled, drawing attention to common spelling patterns.

● Now show the children the text and ask them to identify the three scenes. Model how to read the labels by segmenting the words into phonemes, and looking at the component parts of compound words such as *Headteacher* and *Staffroom*. Look for common spelling patterns, for example: *Staffroom, Cloakroom*.

● Then show the children the unlabelled picture (the differentiated text on the CD-ROM) and ask them to suggest which areas require signs. Discuss whether pictures or words would be more effective. For words, ask the children to sound out the phonemes while you write them down. Remind them who will be visiting the school (parents, workmen, delivery people, other children and other teachers) and encourage them to think about the information that those visitors will need.

Talk, read and write

● Write each label from the text on separate pieces of card, large enough for everyone to be able to see. Ask children to come out and hold the cards and help them to read their cards aloud. Establish the meaning of each word and then put questions to the class such as: *Who is holding the word you would find on a door you are not allowed to go through? Who has the word you would find on the way out? Who has the word for the door of the toilets used by males/females?*

● Ask the children to think of their own questions and encourage them to take turns to ask them to the class. To help children to see the critical features of the words, write the words on the board one by one and ask them to tell you who is holding the card which corresponds with the word.

● Finally, give pairs of children pictures of school printed from differentiated version and ask them to label them using the words which have been modelled.

Extension

Take the children on a walk around the school to find examples of signs and labels, and ask them to make a note of those they see. Back in the classroom, ask them to produce labelled pictures to represent what they have seen. Make a display of their work and use this as a visual aid for future lessons. Where there are signs in languages other than English, draw attention to them and talk about the fact that different languages come from different places.

Ask children to design a sign for the classroom. Remind them to think about the use of colour, typeface, size, using ICT if appropriate. Discuss where the signs should be positioned.

1: 1: T14: to write captions for their own work, such as for display, in class books

1: 1: W10: to recognise the critical features of words, such as length, common spelling patterns and words within words

this would usually be green; colour is important in signs

only important places are signposted; too many signs would be confusing

clear typeface used so that the sign is easy to read

Text © 2007, David Waugh; illustrations © Garry Davies

FIRE EXIT

Headteacher

Hall

Staffroom

Office

Cloakroom

Girls' toilet

Boys' toilet

Main entrance

Key Stage 2

Key Stage 1

too complicated to use an image; word is clearer

positioned at a height that makes it easy for children and adults to read

symbols such as arrows may be used on signs to show the direction

1: 1: T12: to read and use captions, such as labels around the school, on equipment

1: 1: T16: to write and draw simple instructions and labels for everyday classroom use, such as in role play area, for equipment

Walkers' map

by Claire Head

Background

This text introduces map-reading skills and so relates to geography and maths. It provides a simple explanation of the purpose of maps and an example of how symbols are used. Children will enjoy solving the clues and following the trail. The text could perhaps lead to a treasure hunt or literacy walk around the local area.

What's on the CD-ROM

This simpler version focuses attention on the map symbols. The text is best used with small groups. This version can also be used as a writing frame.

Discussing the text

● Tell the class that maps and signs use words and symbols to help people find their way. Ask the children if they have ever used a map or seen someone using a map.

● Read the first paragraph and ask the children to find out what they can see on the map. Give them a few minutes to think, pair and share their ideas. Some children may have more experience than others when it comes to map reading, and taking feedback at this point will allow those children to become the experts! It will also expose misconceptions that you can remedy during the lesson.

● Next, draw attention to the key at the side of the map and read the text that explains the purpose of this. You might first like to mask the key definitions (leaving the pictures uncovered) so that the children can guess what each symbol means and identify it on the map.

● Talk about why map makers use this sort of shorthand. Explain that symbols on a map are used to represent types of places. This is a neater, shorter way of labelling so that the map is not cluttered by too many words. The icons can also be quicker to 'read' and are easier to distinguish from each other.

● Read the rest of the text and ask the children to help you decode the signposts. Establish the meanings of the words *trail*, *picnic* and *footpath*. Ask the children if they have ever been on a walk in the countryside and seen signs like these. It might be more interesting and meaningful for the children if you can talk about your own 'walking' experiences. (Bring in your muddy walking boots, socks, walking stick, compass, photographs, some maps and so on.)

Talk, read and write

● During guided group work ask children to follow the walkers' trail with their fingers. Pause to talk about each significant place that the walkers' pass on route. As you do so, encourage children to use the key to identify each symbol. Ask some targeted questions about the route, for example: *What did the walkers find when they crossed the first bridge?*

● Give the children large flashcards with the names from the map on them and ask them to suggest the sort of landscape the words might describe, for example *Greenside*: grassy hill; *Deep Beck*: deep river or stream.

● Enlarge and cut up the key and place the word cards in a bag. Ask individuals from a group to draw out one word at a time, read it to the group and identify it on the map. Once children are familiar with this game it can be played as a version of map bingo. (You can use the differentiated version of the text to make the necessary resources.)

● More able learners might be ready to talk about the grid-reference features of the map. You will need to explain how each part of the area covered by the map is divided into sections using a grid so that specific places can be pinpointed. This could be linked to geography and maths work.

Extension

Ask children to create a pictorial map of a walkers' route around the school grounds. The focus should be on creating symbols and images that reflect different features, and on considering what aspects of the school grounds pupils or visitors may enjoy visiting.

1: 1: T13: to read and follow simple instructions, such as for classroom routines, lists for groups in workbooks

compass shows which way is north; helps to orientate the walker

simple explanation

question to encourage interaction with the map

technical vocabulary

key explains symbols and icons used on the map

compound word (clue to meaning: 'foot' and 'path')

title in bold

talks directly to the reader; draws them in

example of a simple pictorial map

illustrations support text and provide examples

1: 1: T12: to read and use captions, such as labels around the school, on equipment

1: 1: W10: to recognise the critical features of words, such as length, common spelling patterns and words within words

Walkers' map

If you go walking in the countryside you need a map to help you find your way. What can you see on this walkers' map?

Use the symbols and words at the side of the map to help you follow the walkers' trail. This is called a key and all maps have one.

Information point
Golf course
Camp site
Picnic area
Start of trail
Mountain bike hire

Top Scar
Church
Dale Farm
High Bank
Deep Beck
YHA
Greenside

A B C D E F G H I

5 4 3 2 1

Sometimes, when you are out in the countryside, you see signs like these:

Footpath
Youth Hostel 2 Miles
Picnic Area
Cycle Trail

These signs help you to find paths to specific sites or places of interest.

Text © 2007, Claire Head; photos © 2006, Jupiter Images Corporation

Fantastic offers on garden tools!

by David Waugh

Background

This advertising flyer provides opportunities for labelling and can be a starting point for simple sentence writing. If you can, provide further examples of similar texts and ensure children understand the £ symbol. This text links to calculations and money work in maths.

What's on the CD-ROM

The differentiated text contains the pictures from the core text but each is individually labelled. It omits any reference to the price, instead it focuses on matching the name and picture of each object which can help clarify the information from the core text.

Discussing the text

● Look at the flyer with the children and ask if they have seen anything similar elsewhere, such as in newspapers or magazines. Elicit that the text is an advertisement designed to persuade people to buy garden tools.

● Talk about the title and ask why it is in large capital letters. Look too, at the caption/subheading in capitals: *LOOK AT THESE PRICES!* Discuss the use of exclamation marks and the way the design of the flyer catches the reader's eye.

● Look at each picture and ask the children if they can tell you what the items are. Write the words on the board and talk about the critical features of the words such as length and similar spelling patterns (such as *rake* and *spade*). Identify the phonemes and graphemes of which some of the words are made up. The words *hose*, *rake* and *spade* provide an opportunity to look at the effect of the final 'e' in a split-vowel digraph where it changes a short vowel sound into a long one. Practise this with *rake* and show that it would be pronounced *r-a-k* (to rhyme with *rack*) without the 'e'.

● Together, read the words you have written on the board. Then focus on the words at the foot of the flyer. Can the children match the words on the board to those on the advert? Can they then match the words to the pictures? Drawing on the children's responses, link the image of each tool to its name and price. Occasionally make a mistake to keep children alert and to encourage them to read the words carefully.

Talk, read and write

● Go over the information given in the text and ask the children to practise sentences which use mathematical language. For example, *A lawn mower costs more than a rake* or *A fork costs the same as a spade*. Write up some of these sentences, highlighting the correct use of capital letters and full stops.

● Provide the children with some incomplete sentences as starting points for them to complete using information from the flyer. For example: *The ___ costs £5. The ___ costs £100. The hose pipe costs ____.*

● The most able learners might be able to create their own sentences too. Encourage them to include other comparative words such as *cheap, cheaper* and *cheapest*, and *most expensive*.

● Go on to look at some other features of advertisements, such as placing words like *only, just* and *from* in front of prices. Discuss why advertisers do this, and notice the effect when these words and phrases are added to the core text. Re-read the words *only, just* and *from* and ensure that children can break them down into phonemes and are able to spell them.

● Draw attention to the phrase *Fantastic offers* and discuss persuasive techniques used by advertisers, such as the use of descriptive words and phrases. Ask pairs to invent sentences which make the items in the text sound appealing.

● Ask more able learners to write a shopping list they might take to the garden centre. Print the differentiated text for less able learners and encourage them to role-play different scenarios which involve shopping for the items.

Extension

Ask children to look at home for examples of advertisements which include prices and to bring them into school for display. If you have a home corner in the classroom, create a shop with price lists and ask the children to make posters to advertise goods.

Invite the children to look for prices of items when shopping or looking at newspapers and magazines with parents and carers. Encourage them to make some notes about these so that they can, with your help, write sentences at school.

1: 1: S3: to draw on grammatical awareness, to read with appropriate expression and intonation such as in reading to others, or to dolls, puppets

1: 1: W10: to recognise the critical features of words, such as length, common spelling patterns and words within words

large outline font and capital letters used to catch your eye. Exclamation mark reinforces emphasis

large font and capital letters stand out on page. Exclamation mark reminds you that the items are being sold at low prices

GREEN FINGERS GARDEN CENTRE

FANTASTIC OFFERS ON GARDEN TOOLS!

LOOK AT THESE PRICES!

RAKE	£5	WATERING CAN	£12	SPADE	£6
SHEARS	£15	GRASS RAKE	£7	FORK	£6
WHEEL BARROW	£50	HOSE PIPE	£10	LAWN MOWER	£100

image of item much more eye-catching than text would be

this stands for the word 'pound'

note split vowel digraphs

1: 1: T12: to read and use captions, such as labels around the school, on equipment

1: 1: S8: to begin using full stops to demarcate sentences

1: 1: T14: to write captions for their own work, such as for display, in class books

1: 1: W12: to learn new words from reading and shared experiences, and to make collections of personal interest or significant words and words linked to particular topics

Leaves

by Sally Hewitt

Background

This activity-based text on leaves is a challenging one for Year 1, but useful for introducing hybrid texts and extending vocabulary. The text includes background information and labelled illustrations as well as instructions. It can be used to lead into activities involving sorting and matching, and links well to work in science where children group living things according to observable similarities and differences. It also gives opportunities for developing children's phonic knowledge as they learn to read the names of the leaves. The text can be linked to that on the seed-to-seed cycle of a sunflower, page 40, with the cycle of growth and decay for leaves being presented in a similar format. It could also be linked to 'Create an autumn leaves display' on page 42. The text will be at its most effective if explored during the autumn term when deciduous leaves will be falling and it will be easy for children to find lots of examples. Ideally, provide collections of leaves for the children to see and touch during this lesson.

What's on the CD-ROM

The differentiated text on the CD-ROM is a simplified version of the core text. It contains the same illustrations and labels but has less additional information, so there are fewer reading demands. However, it still retains the investigating instructions, but these have been divided into three simple stages.

Discussing the text

● Read the text to the children and then with them, drawing attention to the layout which includes a title, subheading, text in a circle and labelled pictures of leaves. Help the children to relate the pictures of the different leaves to their names mentioned in the text.

● Talk about some of the interesting information about leaves and, ideally, provide some real examples for the children to examine these features for themselves.

● Focus on the text in the circle and talk about why leaves fall off some trees in the autumn and winter and grow in the spring and summer. Share experiences of seeing trees with changing and falling leaves.

● Discuss the different shapes and forms of the leaves, again examining real ones if possible. Work with the children to write sentences to describe them. Draw attention to the use of capital letters and full stops, and emphasise the concept of a sentence by occasionally producing one which is incomplete for the children to finish.

● Highlight some of the high frequency and CVC words in the text, for example *put, rub, box* and *wax*. Show the children how the words can be segmented into phonemes and graphemes and then blended together when we read them. Look at the words again and ask the children if they can change the first letters/ initial sounds to make different words. For example, *can, man, tan, fan; put, shut, tut, hut, gut; rub, pub, dub, sub; box, fox, cox*. If the children suggest words which have the same rimes but different spellings (for example, *socks* to rhyme with *box*), point this out and explain that the same sound can sometimes be made using different letters.

Talk, read and write

● Provide pairs of children with examples of different kinds of leaves. Model how to ask questions which involve descriptions of the leaves, for example: *This leaf is hard and shiny. It has spiky points. What is it?* Once the children have practised using descriptive language, create a wordbank of useful words.

● Next, ask them to help you to write descriptions of the leaves. Read the descriptions together and talk about how the words are written.

● Look at the cycle of growth and decay for leaves on deciduous trees and show how this can be presented in circular form (similar to that for sunflower seeds, see page 40).

Extension

Ask children to collect clean dry leaves and bring them to school. They can go on to follow the instructions from the text to make rubbings which can be labelled, or could store the leaves and observe them as in the text, to see what happens to them. These observations can form a shared writing activity for a future literacy lesson. After making rubbings, ask the children to think about the process and to help you to write a set of instructions which can be displayed alongside the finished rubbings.

1: 1: T13: to read and follow simple instructions, such as for classroom routines, lists for groups in workbooks

1: 1: S4: to write captions and simple sentences, and to re-read, recognising whether or not they make sense, such as missing words, wrong word order

1: 1: W4: to discriminate and segment all three phonemes in CVC words

draws the reader in

two sets of simple instructions

Text extract from "Plants (Fascinating Science Series)" by Sally Hewitt © 2001, Aladdin Books Ltd (2001, Franklin Watts); photos: background leaves © Penelope Berger, pine leaf © Filip George, horse chestnut leaf © Philip Mamet, oak leaf © Ian Labardee, maple leaf © Chris Root, laurel leaf © Fernando Sanz, holly leaf © Go Vicinity.

Leaves

COMPARE DIFFERENT LEAVES

Collect as many different leaves as you can – deciduous, evergreen, simple and compound. A leaf with one blade – the flat, green part – is a simple leaf. A compound leaf, such as horse chestnut leaf, is made up of several blades. Pine needles are very thin leaves with a tough wax coat that can survive cold winters.

Deciduous trees have big green leaves that collect sunlight in spring and summer. In the autumn when it gets colder, the leaves fall and die. Evergreen trees keep their leaves all year round.

Try making some leaf rubbings. Lay white paper over a leaf with its underside facing upwards. Rub the paper evenly with a wax crayon and see the leaf shape and its raised pattern of veins appear.

Put the leaves in a shoe box and shut the lid. Check them every few days. Do all the leaves dry out and crumble? Do any become 'skeleton' leaves, when all that is left is the veins? Do the evergreen leaves survive the longest?

horse chestnut

oak

maple

pine

holly

laurel

large, bold font for heading

technical vocabulary which is explained in the text

photos extend the information in the text

questions encourage the reader to investigate

1: 1: T12: to read and use captions, such as labels around the school, on equipment

1: 1: W5: to blend phonemes to read CVC words

1: 1: T14: to write captions for their own work, such as for display, in class books

Flowering plants

by Claire Head

Background

This information text can be used in conjunction with practical science work related to planting seeds and growing flowering plants. It introduces certain features of non-fiction texts (such as photographs, glossaries, subheadings) and can help to show children how to locate specific information. This topic could be linked to several other texts and extended to develop a garden centre role-play area in the classroom.

What's on the CD-ROM

This text is a picture of a labelled plant. It will help younger children to understand some of the technical terms used in the core text, especially those terms in the glossary.

Discussing the text

● Tell the children that this is a factual text and not a story. Encourage them to identify the clues that tell the reader that this is an information text (such as the title, subheadings, photographs and glossary). Talk about some of the differences between fiction and non-fiction. Discuss how information texts are based on facts, and discuss the meaning of the word *fact.*

● Read the first paragraph and discuss the facts that have been presented. Ask the children to count the facts that they hear on a second reading. Then look at the text and ask the children to help you count the sentences the author has used – did she have one idea per sentence? Encourage some children to explain how we can recognise a sentence and ask them to highlight the capital letters and full stops. Use the line endings to establish the difference between starting a new line and starting a new sentence.

● Draw attention to the glossary and discuss its purpose – to give us more information about plants. Point to each part of the photograph of the plant and ask the children to identify it. Suggest that they could do this by reading the glossary or by drawing on their own knowledge and experience. Can any of the children suggest an alternative word instead of *stem* (such as *stalk*)? Use the differentiated text to model this process, if required.

● Tell the children that you are going to ask them some questions about the extract and you want to know how, by using the text and pictures, they can locate the information needed to answer. Ask, for example: *Which part of the plant is underground? What does the stem do for the plant? What do plants need to live and grow?* Discuss how the glossary can be a useful starting point.

Talk, read and write

● Ask the children to draw a flowering plant and label it. The differentiated version of the text can be used to support less able learners with this task.

● Make large flashcards using the glossary words. Ask children to choose one and give an oral definition of the word. Alternatively, mix up words and definitions and ask the children to match them up again.

● Make a cloze procedure activity by deleting or hiding specific words (you could use the editable text from the CD-ROM), for example high frequency words, specialised terminology, verbs, nouns, words key to comprehension. Children could help you to replace the words in shared or guided reading groups. Some children may be able to do this independently on the computer.

● Make a list of the flowering plants that children know by name. Use real plants, and photographs (for example from gardening magazines) to stimulate further research. Encourage the children to talk about the differences and similarities they find. Then ask them to work together to create a plant A–Z, for example *Aa anemone, Bb bluebell…*

● In pairs, ask the children to tell each other what they have learned about how plants grow. They could use the glossary to help with their explanations, or you could write headings on the board to provide talking prompts.

Extension

Ask children to look closely at any flowering plants they see at or near home. If possible, lend them a magnifying glass and let them be flower detectives. Encourage children to draw or describe in detail the plants that they have observed. Remind children not to pick any plants that they see growing.

Flowering plants

Flowering plants grow towards the sun. Light from the sun helps plants to make food. The roots of the plant suck up water and minerals found in the soil. The roots also help to hold the plant firmly in the ground.

What do plants need to live and grow?

Plants need air, sunlight, water and soil to help them grow.
There are all kinds of flowering plants in different colours, shapes and sizes.

Photo © 2006, Jupiter Images Corporation

Glossary
Leaves – plants spread out their green leaves to catch sunlight to give the plant energy to grow and live.
Petal – colourful scented petals attract insects and birds to the flower.
Roots – these grow down into the soil and suck up water and food.
Soil – this contains water and nutrients for the plant. Dead leaves, rotting plants and insects enrich the soil.
Stem – this is a thin tube that supports the plant and allows water and minerals to travel up to the leaves and petals.

Do you know the names of any flowering plants?

1: 1: W12: to learn new words from reading and shared experiences

1: 1: S5: to recognise full stops and capital letters

title in larger font

introduction contains definition of flowering plants

question used to help the reader locate information

picture-prompts to stimulate further discussion and provide visual information

1: 1: S7: to know that a line of writing is not necessarily the same as a sentence

1: 1: T16: to write and draw simple instructions and labels

simple present tense; formal style used

sub-headings and glossary are features of information texts

precise, technical vocabulary

1: 1: S6: to begin using the term sentence

Christmas in Europe

by David Waugh

Background

This pictorial text shows a map of Europe with captions linked to certain countries, telling the reader when gifts are exchanged at Christmas and what a typical Christmas meal might contain. The activity suggested below involves looking at a map and reading labels, as well as finding out information about festivals. It can be linked to work in geography (using globes, maps and plans at a range of scales, and knowledge and understanding of places), and to festivals and celebrations in RE.

What's on the CD-ROM

The differentiated text on the CD-ROM includes similar information, but for different countries. Like the core text the information is presented in boxes with the country's flag. However the map is omitted and information is written in full sentences. This enables comparisons to be drawn between different ways of presenting information.

Discussing the text

● Begin by inviting the children to share their experiences of celebrating festivals, from exchanging gifts to wearing special clothes and eating special meals. Some children from non-Christian cultures may not take part in festivities at Christmas time, but will be interested to find out about and compare Christmas festivities with those which they take part in.

● Look at the map and ask the children to locate the country in which they live. Encourage them to point out other countries which they either recognise or are able to work out how to pronounce phonically, for example *Spain*, *France*, *Norway*, *Denmark*, *Italy*, *Finland* and *Iceland*.

● Now draw attention to the captions on the map. Explain that the text boxes show certain countries' flags and provide brief information about their Christmas traditions. Find *Spain* on the map and ask the children if they can tell you when gifts are exchanged. They may be interested to see that this is generally much later than in the United Kingdom. Talk with them about when they exchange gifts and then compare this with the information in the other text boxes. (You may need to remind children that Christmas day is 25 December and

Christmas Eve is 24 December.)

● Discuss typical meals which the children eat at Christmas and at other festivals and then ask the children to look at the caption boxes to find out about Christmas meals in other countries. Talk about some of the dishes which may be unfamiliar such as *truffles*, *herring*, *mutton* and *broth*, ideally showing the children photographs of such foods to aid understanding.

Talk, read and write

● Look at the differentiated text on the CD-ROM, and read some of the sentences. Model how this information could be added to the map, in the form of those already on the map with abbreviated 'shorthand' sentences.

● By contrast, demonstrate how some of the information from the text boxes on the core text could be written as full sentences. Re-read one of the full sentences you have just abbreviated to reinforce this. Pay particular attention to the use of full stops, which are missing from the note format used in the labels.

● Guide children as they read other sentences and extract information to place in text boxes. Talk about the key words and help them to read the sentences. Discuss the spellings of the foods and look for opportunities to reinforce and develop phonic knowledge by looking at common spelling patterns.

● Write some names of countries on card or on the board and ask the children to look for matching names of countries on the map. Notice how the names on the map are in full capitals while those which you write have a capital only for the first letter. Elicit that each country has an initial capital because it is a name, relating this to the children's names. Discuss the reason for the full capitals on the map. (It makes the country names stand out and so easier to read.)

Extension

Ask children to find out more about Christmas traditions in other parts of the world. Ask children from non-Christian faiths to find out details about their celebrations across the globe so that a world map can be displayed with text boxes of information about festivals around the world.

1: 1: T12: to read and use captions

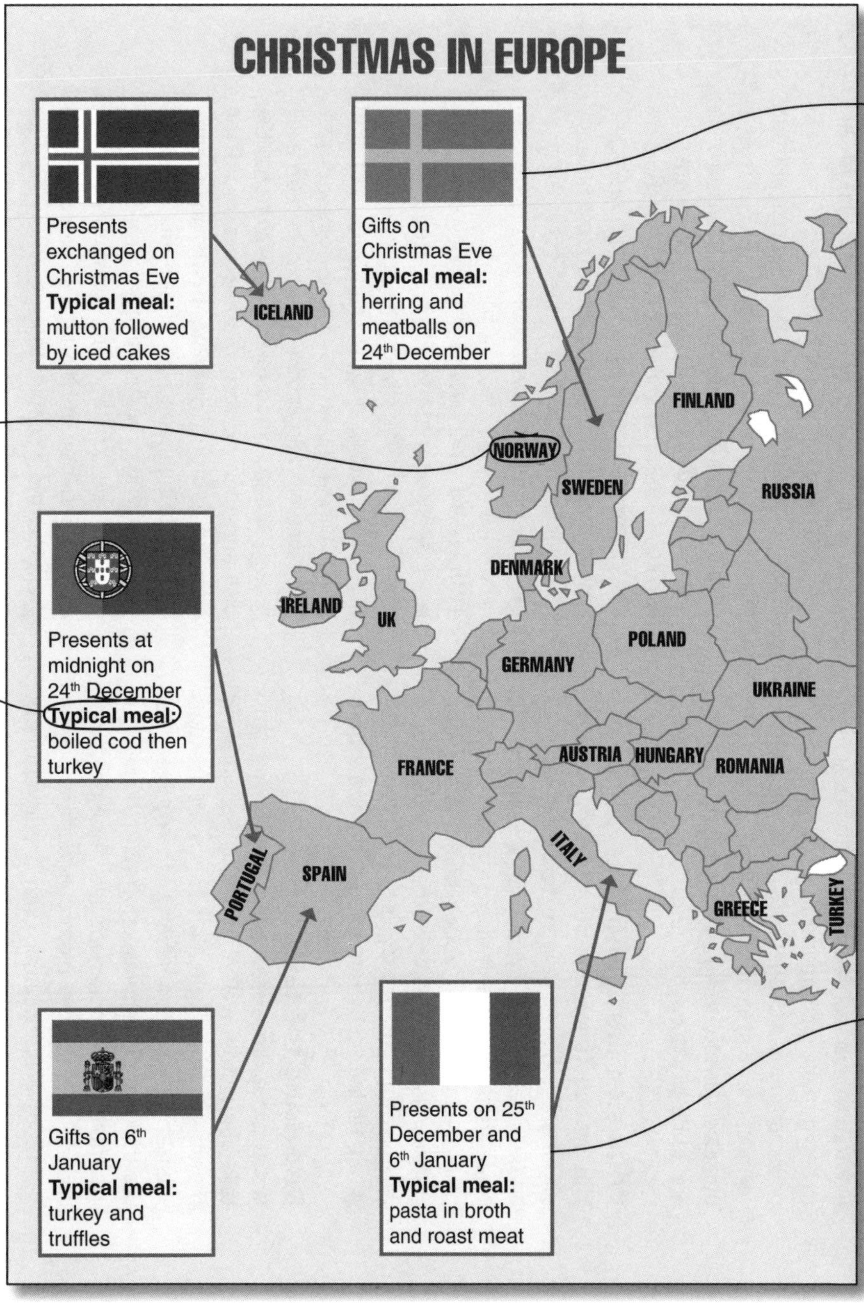

no capital letter or full stop shows that these are not full sentences

1: 1: S9: to use a capital letter for the personal pronoun 'I' and for the start of a sentence

each text box includes the same type of information (presents; food)

Text © 2007, David Waugh; flags © Nova Developments

CHRISTMAS IN EUROPE

Gifts on Christmas Eve
Typical meal: herring and meatballs on 24th December

Presents exchanged on Christmas Eve
Typical meal: mutton followed by iced cakes

ICELAND

NORWAY

SWEDEN

FINLAND

RUSSIA

DENMARK

UK

IRELAND

GERMANY

POLAND

AUSTRIA **HUNGARY**

UKRAINE

ROMANIA

FRANCE

ITALY

GREECE

TURKEY

PORTUGAL

SPAIN

Presents on 25th December and 6th January
Typical meal: pasta in broth and roast meat

Presents at midnight on 24th December
Typical meal: boiled cod then turkey

Gifts on 6th January
Typical meal: turkey and truffles

bold capital typeface for names of countries

key words are in bold to make them stand out

1: 1: T14: to write captions for their own work, such as for display, in class books

1: 1: S8: to begin using full stops to demarcate sentences

How do we move? by Anita Ganeri

Background

This attractive visual text provides information about how humans are able to move. The text is presented in different forms: short questions encourage the reader to relate theory to practice and reflect on how the body feels in action, while simple statements provide information about specific joints and bones. The use of a composite photograph and diagram will appeal to children and allow them to begin making comparisons of different types of visual image. This extract could be used in connection with cross-curricular topics on ourselves, living things and keeping healthy, and in PE practice.

What's on the CD-ROM

This writing frame requires children to relate information from the core text to their own bodies, and will particularly appeal to kinaesthetic learners. It also provides a starting point for discussion about being active and staying healthy. The chart can be used as a writing frame for individuals to complete or as a group record sheet with you acting as a scribe.

Discussing the text

● Look at the extract with the children and talk about the way that the information is presented. Draw attention to layout features such as the diagram, labels with key lines, key words in bold, and discuss how it makes the information easy for the reader to understand. Look closely at the picture and note how it combines a photograph with a diagram. Ask the children to suggest why this makes the illustration interesting to look at.

● Ask the children what they notice about the title. How can the children tell it is a question? Why has the author used a question? It intrigues the reader and encourages him or her to think about the information that follows.

● Before reading the text, briefly explain the difference between bones and muscles.

● Ask the children to think, pair and share with a partner to explain why we need bones under the skin. Ask a few pairs to feed back, and point out that hearing things explained in different ways helps us to understand better and learn new information.

● Now read the labels with the children. As you read the two questions, ask the children to attempt each action and then describe what it feels like.

● Using the editable text, remove some of the capital letters and full stops in the description. Firstly, focus on the language features of the questions by drawing attention to the question mark, then explain that some of the other punctuation was 'accidentally' left off the text. Ask volunteers to add the missing capital letters at the start of sentences, and the missing full stops at the end. Ask whether punctuation is required for the labels on the right hand side of the illustration. Why not?

● Model writing the following question on the board: *What does your body feel like?* Ensure that the children have understood any new vocabulary, and can use words such as *bend* and *shorten* in sentences.

Talk, read and write

● Display or print the differentiated text from the CD-ROM. Talk about the action words in the table: *jump, hop, bounce, clap, sit* and *stand*. Play a game with the children using a large dice with an action word written on each face. Children should take it in turns to roll the dice and then demonstrate the action for the class or a group (miming bouncing a ball). Encourage children to talk about which muscles they are using in each activity.

● Ask the children to draw themselves actively engaged in one type of exercise. Help them to write a caption to explain how they are moving and using the body.

Extension

Assist the children with taking digital photographs of each other playing PE games or sports. (Obtain parents' and carers' permission before taking photographs.) Use these action shots as a display or class book with captions written by the children.

1: 1: S4: to write captions and simple sentences, and to re-read, recognising whether or not they make sense, such as missing words, wrong word order

use of question form; involves and engages reader

1: 1: S9: to use a capital letter for the personal pronoun 'I' and for the start of a sentence

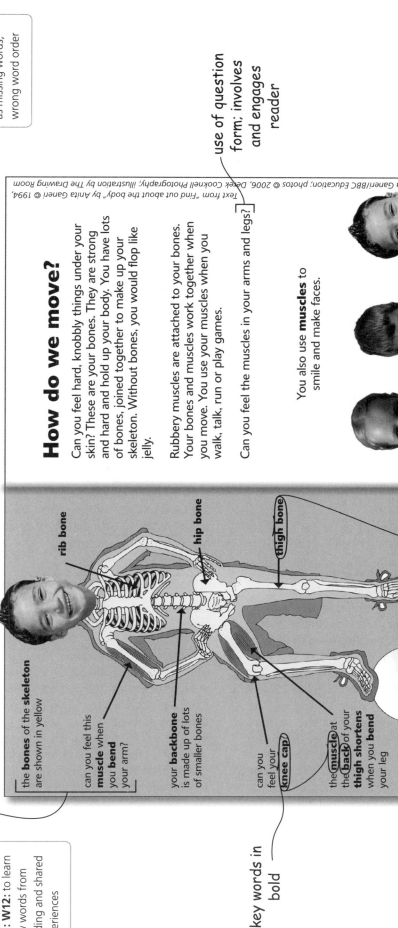

Text from "Find out about the body" by Anita Ganeri © 1994, Anita Ganeri/BBC Education; photos © 2006, Derek Cooknell Photography; illustration by The Drawing Room

How do we move?

Can you feel hard, knobbly things under your skin? These are your bones. They are strong and hard and hold up your body. You have lots of bones, joined together to make up your skeleton. Without bones, you would flop like jelly.

Rubbery muscles are attached to your bones. Your bones and muscles work together when you move. You use your muscles when you walk, talk, run or play games.

Can you feel the muscles in your arms and legs?

You also use **muscles** to smile and make faces.

the **bones** of the **skeleton** are shown in yellow

rib bone

can you feel this **muscle** when you **bend** your arm?

hip bone

your **backbone** is made up of lots of smaller bones

thigh bone

can you feel your **knee cap**?

the **muscle** at the **back** of your **thigh shortens** when you **bend** your leg

some labels just point to parts of the body, and don't include other information

some information is given in simple sentences

key words in bold

1: 1: T14: to write captions for their own work, such as for display, in class books

1: 1: W12: to learn new words from reading and shared experiences

1: 1: S8: to begin using full stops to demarcate sentences

Clothes

by Claire Head

Background

You can use this extract as a springboard for work on captions and lists. Cross-curricular links could be made to science and geography with related work about materials and their properties, and the weather and climate. Children can be introduced to some common features found in information texts: technical vocabulary; questions; labelled pictures; and will be able to draw on personal experience to interact with the text.

What's on the CD-ROM

This text is a simplified version of the core text. The explanation is omitted to reduce reading demands. The four children's dilemmas are still included, as are the pictures of clothing, there are also labels for these clothes and others. Less able leaners could label these items and draw pictures of appropriate items of clothing, while more able learners could create labelled and captioned diagrams.

Discussing the text

● Introduce the concept of selecting clothes by asking them to comment on the clothes they are wearing today, and why they are wearing them. If necessary, prompt the children by asking them what the weather is like today.

● Explain that this text is about making choices about what clothes people should wear. In order to do this, they need to find out what each of the people will be doing.

● Read the first two sentences and ask the children to share ideas about suitable clothes for different kinds of weather. Discuss why we wear different clothes in different seasons. Then talk about wearing clothes for other purposes, for example playing sport, and discuss why special clothing is often required. Explore the need for protective clothing such as a bicycle helmet, or an apron for cooking.

● Read the question in the third paragraph and point out the question mark. Explain that information books give us answers and explain things *and* they often use questions that prompt the reader to think about the information as this helps people to learn.

● Ask a child to choose one of the children shown in the text and help you to read the clue about the clothes this child might need.

Encourage children to identify suitable pictures. On a subsequent reading, you could ask the children to help you write labels for the clothing. Repeat the process by reading each clue with the children and asking them to give reasons for their choices as you list them.

● Finally, ask if they can add anything else to each list. For example: *When you go out in cold weather what do you wear? Is it on the list?*

Talk, read and write

● Use the text to make a writing frame for the children. Blank out the pictures of the children and ask the children to draw themselves in the spaces. Challenge the children to explain what they would wear for different activities or in different types of weather and write explanatory captions.

● Use the table below to play a guessing game with the class or guided groups. For example, *I am wearing a helmet, some knee pads, a pair of special leather gloves… What am I doing?* If possible, bring in real examples of these clothes and peg them on a washing line after taking each item from a mystery bag.

Activities	Clothing
Painting a picture	Apron, old shirt
Skateboarding	Helmet, knee pads, elbow pads, gloves
Going to bed	Pyjamas/nightshirt, slippers, dressing gown

● After playing this game, hand out the items of clothing to the children. Ask them to take it in turns to explain the purpose of the piece of clothing, and how this is linked to the design and type of material.

● You could also ask the children to sort items of clothing into different containers, for example clothes that keep us dry/warm; for school/sport and give reasons for their choices.

Extension

Talk to the children about clothing for special occasions. Suggest to the children that they ask their families and friends to tell them about special clothes that they have worn for memorable occasions. If possible, encourage the children to bring in photographs and use these to tell other children about why the outfits being worn are special.

1: 1: T15: to make simple lists for planning, reminding, and so on

1: 1: S4: to write captions and simple sentences, and to re-read, recognising whether or not they make sense, such as missing words, wrong word order

title in large bold font for emphasis

question mark to draw the reader in

repeated question

Clothes

We wear different sorts of clothes for different purposes. Some clothes help to keep us warm by trapping heat, made by our bodies, next to the skin.

Clothes we choose to wear when it is warm and sunny are light on the skin and help to keep us cool.

Sometimes we need to wear special clothing that protects us. Can you think of any reasons why someone might need to dress in protective clothing?

It is important to choose the right kind of clothing to wear for everything you do in every kind of weather! Can you help these children choose the best clothes to wear?

I am going to play outside but I need to wrap up warm as it is very cold today. What shall I wear?

I am going to walk to the shop with my dad. It's raining but I don't care. I love jumping in the puddles! What shall I wear?

I am going on holiday. It will be sunny and hot. I can't wait to go swimming! What shall I take with me to wear?

I am going to ride my bike to my friend's house. I need to make sure I stay safe. What shall I wear?

introductory sentences telling you what the text is going to be about

exclamation mark to emphasise the importance of choosing the right clothes

personal pronoun starts each sentence. Tells you that each person is telling you about themselves

1: 1: T14: to write captions for their own work, such as for display, in class books

1: 1: W10: to recognise the critical features of words, such as length, common spelling patterns and words within words

Fruit

by Claire Head

Background

This text provides a visual introduction to lists and offers simple facts about fruit. The topic links to geography (fruits from around the world); maths (halving and quartering, counting, simple Venn diagrams, bar charts); science (planting citrus pips, healthy eating); and design and technology ('Eat more fruit and vegetables' QCA Unit 1C). The text will serve as a stimulus to help children create a fruit salad shopping list to tie in with the fruit salad recipe on page 36.

What's on the CD-ROM

This simple grid can be used as a writing frame or talk-for-writing frame to help children collect information about six of the fruits. Information could be found from the extract, other reference material and children's knowledge and experience. The chart could be edited and used to match and label different fruits or to collect information about children's favourite fruits.

Discussing the text

● Begin by asking the children how many fruits they can name. Challenge the class to work together to beat a target number of fruits. Ask pairs to feed back, and list all their ideas on the board.

● Introduce the text by telling the children that you are going to compare their list to a list from a book. Show the text and read the first subheading and introductory paragraph.

● Ask the children to scan the text to see if they recognise any words from their fruit list. During feedback, point out that the fruits are grouped together for a specific reason. Explain that the author has organised the fruits in lists that match the subheadings: *Citrus fruits*, for example, all have something in common.

● Notice how the layout and presentation of the text – for example bold text, subheadings and pictures – helps the reader to locate information. Read the information to the children and encourage talk about what these fruits taste like.

● Cover the list of tree fruits and ask the children to name fruits that they think grow on trees. Then check to see if they are on the list. Talk about the question the text asks about tree fruit (*Which fruits contain stones?*) and ask the children to consider how they can find out. If possible, bring in examples of tree fruits, and cut them open during the lesson to reveal the stone.

● Once children have become familiar with the content and meaning of the text, use it to highlight specific words and spelling patterns. For example, ask the children what they notice about the words in the *Berries* list.

Talk, read and write

● During guided group work identify words containing specific phonemes and spelling patterns, depending on the ability of each group, for example: initial phonemes 'b', 'a' and 'l'; consonant clusters 'gr', 'bl', 'cr' and 'str'; consonant digraph 'ch'; medial vowel phonemes 'ea' and 'oo'; plurals *apple* '+s', *banana* '+s', and *berry* '–y' and '+ies'.

● Provide real examples of the fruit where possible. In groups, ask the children to choose one fruit from the text to describe. Encourage the children to use their senses, their experience and the information learned from reading the extract. After some oral rehearsal, ask the children to write simple sentences about their chosen fruit. For example, *This fruit is small, red and juicy. It is a type of berry. It grows on a plant and has some green leaves on the top.* These descriptions can be turned into riddles, by adding *What is it?*, and used in a fruit quiz during the plenary, subsequent lessons or as part of a display.

● Return to the text, and read the final questions (*Have you ever eaten fruit salad…?*). In groups, ask the children to discuss which fruit they would like to include in a fruit salad. They should then write a shopping list for the fruit salad, remembering to state how many items of each fruit are required.

Extension

Ask children to try to find out which countries the fruit they buy comes from. Can they bring in any labels they have saved?

Ask family and friends if they can tell children about unusual fruits with unusual names for adding to the class fruit list.

Keep a class list of all the different types of fruit that the children eat during a week.

Text © 2007, Claire Head; photos © 2006, Jupiter Images Corporation

FRUIT

What is a fruit?

A fruit is the fleshy part of a plant that contains its seeds. It can be eaten. All fruits should be washed before you eat them. Some fruits need to be peeled before you eat them.

All kinds of fruits

Tree fruits

Some of these fruits contain stones in the middle. Do you know which ones?

Apple
Apricot
Cherry
Fig
Peach
Pear
Plum

Citrus fruits

Citrus fruits contain pips. These can be planted and some will eventually grow into trees.

Grapefruit
Lemon
Lime
Orange

Tropical and exotic fruits

These grow best in hot countries.

Banana
Mango
Papaya
Pineapple

Berries

These soft fruits grow on plants or small bushes. They have many small seeds.

Bilberry
Blackberry
Blueberry
Cranberry
Raspberry
Strawberry

Have you ever eaten fruit salad? Which fruits would you include in a fruit salad?

1: 1: T15: to make simple lists for planning, reminding, and so on

main heading in large bold typeface

questions reader to encourage further investigation

technical vocabulary

pictures support text and provide additional information

1: 1: W10: to recognise the critical features of words, such as length, common spelling patterns and words within words

1: 1: T1: to reinforce and apply their word-level skills through shared and guided reading

introduction answers the sub-heading; explains what the text is about

category sub-heading flagged up in bold, red typeface

list format; words listed in alphabetical order

question to appeal directly to the reader to promote further research and interest

1: 1: S4: to write captions and simple sentences

My food diary

by Claire Head

Background

This text shows how information can be presented in a variety of formats. The chart provides a summary of a child's food intake over a one week period, and additional information is provided in the form of a journal extract and illustrations. Some of the data has not yet been entered on the chart, allowing children to use supplementary texts to add information. This text links well with work on healthy eating and school dinners.

What's on the CD-ROM

The CD-ROM contains a blank chart for one day which children can use to create their own food diary. The healthy food pyramid can be used to scaffold conversations about the importance of eating a balanced diet. Explain how a balanced diet reflects the ratio of food groups in the pyramid, and then ask the children to use it to tell a friend about the food groups they have eaten during the day.

Discussing the text

● Explain that this chart lists everything Sam had to eat over the course of a school week. Point to the row and column headings as you explain how Sam recorded the information. Check the children understand by asking a range of questions (such as: *What did Sam have for breakfast on Monday?*) and model how to locate the answers in the chart.

● Create true or false statement cards from the information in the chart and play a game of 'true or false?'. For example, *On Wednesday Sam had a jacket potato with baked beans for his tea.* (True.) *On Wednesday Sam had raspberry yoghurt for his breakfast.* (False.)

● Point out to the children that the last column in the chart, which shows us what sort of snacks Sam ate, contains pictures instead of words. Ask the children to help you identify and label the snacks. Model how to enter the information into the chart as text. Ask the children to spell out words as you add them.

● Encourage the children to talk about the snacks they eat at playtime or at home. Discuss healthy snacks such as fruit and less healthy alternatives such as crisps or chocolate. To extend children's thinking, ask them to use the chart to identify all the fruit that Sam ate

throughout the week, including as part of a meal.

● Draw attention to the two empty boxes on the chart and explain that Sam forgot to fill these in. Ask for suggestions on where the missing information might be found. Together, read the page from Sam's journal and ask the children to think about which key words need to be entered into the chart (*fish, chips, ice cream*) and for which day (*Thursday*).

● Ask the children what they think Sam had for lunch on Tuesday. What do they usually have for lunch? Who has school dinners or packed lunch? Stress that there is no correct answer to this question. You could develop this into a discussion on healthy eating.

Talk, read and write

● Ask the class or group if they can remember what Sam's favourite meal is? Then use circle time to allow the children to share their preferences using the sentence prompt *My favourite food is…* Then, in guided writing help the children to write this sentence and add labelled illustrations as a form of planning for writing.

● Play, 'In my lunch box today I have…' where the next person repeats then adds another item. Following this oral rehearsal most children will be ready to draw and label the contents of their ideal lunch box. Alternatively, ask the children to list the items they would need for a picnic in the park. This activity works well in a role-play area where children can pack a real picnic basket.

● Ask the children to make a menu for that day's school dinner. Create a writing frame with headings such as main course, pudding and drinks, and model how to capture information. The menu could be used in the role-play area to support speaking and listening activities.

Extension

Encourage children to ask members of their family about their favourite foods.

Ask children to keep a food diary for a week. Parents or carers may need to offer support with filling in the diary at home.

heading in bold

no capital letters or full stops used for food diary entries; these are not full sentences

pictures and text used to present information

signals missing information

My Food Diary

Day of the week	Breakfast	Lunch	Tea-time	Snacks
Monday	a bowl of cereal	two tuna and cucumber sandwiches	vegetable curry and rice	
Tuesday	one slice of toast with jam	?	fish pie with roast potatoes and broccoli	
Wednesday	a strawberry yoghurt	salad and chicken in pitta bread pockets	a jacket potato with baked beans	
Thursday	a bowl of cereal	three vegetable samosas	?	
Friday	two slices of toast with peanut butter	pasta with tomatoes, ham and onion	omelette with chips and peas	
Saturday	a boiled egg with toasted soldiers	fruit salad	pizza with tomatoes, cheese and pineapple	
Sunday	three pancakes with maple syrup	roast chicken with mashed potatoes, carrots, and parsnips	banana sandwiches and a yoghurt	

On Thursday I went out for my tea with my Grandma and Grandad. We had fish and chips. I had tomato sauce with mine! This is my favourite food. I had some ice-cream with a cherry on top for pudding. Yum!

Text © 2007, Claire Head; photos © 2006, Jupiter Images Corporation

days of the week begin with a capital letter

precise number specified to make diary more accurate

full sentences in journal

Shopping list

by David Waugh

Background

A shopping list is one of the most familiar types of list, and provides an excellent opportunity for speaking and listening and writing activities linked to role play. The example that has been provided can be added to by teachers and children as appropriate to current topics and to include favourites. The items listed here are generally phonically regular and should all be familiar to most children. The list includes plurals and some information such as size, colour, number and type of certain items. The text can be discussed in the context of other lists with which the children may be familiar, as well as simple songs such as 'The Twelve Days of Christmas'. The list might be studied in conjunction with lists of names, lists in books and newspapers and lists around the classroom and the school.

What's on the CD-ROM

The differentiated text is a simpler and shorter version of a shopping list, with pictures of the items presented next to the names to aid children's recognition and understanding. The differentiated list can be used to support role-play activities, and to provide a model for children's own writing. Children could also use a cut up version to play simple 'Snap' or sorting games.

Discussing the text

● Explain to the children that they are going to look at a list. Ask them if they know what a list is and why one might be made. If they can see examples of lists in the classroom, draw attention to these. There might be, for example, lists of classroom rules, lists of names, lists of things to do.

● Now show the children the shopping list. Talk to them about the way in which the text is set out, one item under another. Point out that the items are listed fairly randomly and they are not in alphabetical order. Discuss different ways in which the list might have been set out. For example, some people make shopping lists for supermarket shopping which take into account where in the shop each item can be found so that they can move from aisle to aisle without having to retrace their steps.

● Read the full list with the children and model how to segment and blend unfamiliar words to decode them. You might, initially, draw some of the items next to their names to help the children to recognise the items.

● Now say some of the names of items at random and ask the children to take turns to come out and point to the appropriate words. Emphasise the initial sound in words to support the matching of the spoken words to the written ones.

● Talk about the items which have additional details given in brackets, such as the number, size or type. Ask the children to look at all of the items and to suggest details which might be useful to know for other items, for example the variety and/or colour of apples, the size of carrots, the type of cabbage. Write some of these ideas on the board and discuss spelling and ways of presenting the information. Talk with the children about the use of details in brackets. Why do they think the author did this? (The most important part of the information – the food item – is given first; the other information is *supplementary*.)

Talk, read and write

● Rehearse the language and behaviour that shoppers use, and ask the children to use the lists in the role-play area.

● Print and cut up the lists, and ask the children to sort them into different categories, such as fruit and veg, dairy and so on.

● Ask the children to suggest other items for the list. Write some of these on the board with the children's help.

● Explore other occasions when children might create a list, for example a wish list for a birthday, or ingredients for a special meal. Discuss how the list could be presented, and allow the children to create their own pictorial or written list.

Extension

Ask children to discuss with parents and carers the shopping lists they use. Encourage them to ask for copies to share with the class. Ask them to make lists at home. These might be shopping lists or could be lists of favourite toys, books or television programmes.

1: 1: T15: to make simple lists for planning, reminding, and so on

1: 1: W12: to learn new words from reading and shared experiences, and to make collections of personal interest or significant words and words linked to particular topics

day of week to remind shopper which list this is – could have been jotted down over several days

specifies type of bread

reminds shopper of number of items required (perhaps for a recipe?)

Text © 2007, David Waugh, photo © 2006, Jupiter Images Corporation

SHOPPING LIST
(MONDAY)
6 eggs
fish fingers
carrots
apples
potatoes (small)
lettuce
cabbage
oranges
bread (brown sliced)
milk (2 bottles)
butter
beans (2 cans)
sweetcorn
orange juice (3 cartons)
bag of crisps

simple plural ending

listed one under another to allow shopper to scan items quickly. Random order of items

list is 'handwritten' onto a notepad so it can be torn out and taken shopping

CVC word

1: 1: T13: to read and follow simple instructions, such as for classroom routines, lists for groups in workbooks

1: 1: W10: to recognise the critical features of words, such as length, common spelling patterns and words within words

School dinner menu by Scholastic Ltd

Background

The text focuses on one week's school dinner menu in a local authority which has given high priority to healthy eating. The foods will be familiar to most children, although many of the words themselves are likely to be challenging to read. The text will work well in conjunction with 'Shopping list' on page 32 and can be linked to work in PSHE on healthy eating, and to science.

What's on the CD-ROM

The differentiated text on the CD-ROM takes the foods from Monday's menu and sets them out in a more conventional 'menu' format. This can be used to support role-play activities around making choices and ordering food. Children could also use it as a model for creating their own 'dream' menu.

Discussing the text

● Look at the menu with the children and read it to them. Discuss the presentation and ask children if they have seen menus before and, if so, where. Highlight the difference between this menu (which shows a whole week's menu plan) and a restaurant-style format.

● Discuss the way in which items are presented so that customers can make choices. Explain that the menu is not a list of all the foods which each person will eat. Point out that main courses and desserts and drinks are separated from each other. Note familiar words such as *with* and *or* and explain that *or* is used to show where there is a choice between two items. Elsewhere in the menu there are lists of alternatives with no conjunctions to separate them.

● Look at some of the words which children may not have seen written down before such as *Homemade*, *Jacket*, *Apricot* and *Yoghurt* and show the children how these can be broken up into phonemes to help the reader to sound them and read them.

● After looking at the menu, ask the children to think, pair and share their ideas for other items for a menu, then ask them to take turns to make suggestions for you to write on the board. Model the writing and talk aloud to show the children the thought processes which a writer may use. For example: *I need to use a capital letter at the beginning. Now I'm writing a different item I'll need to start a new line.*

● Discuss how words might be spelled by referring to sounds and demonstrate that many words can be constructed by saying them out loud and breaking them into phonemes which can be represented by graphemes.

Talk, read and write

● Together, look at the differentiated text which shows a 'typical' menu layout, and compare the differences between this and the core text. The main difference is that the school menu is for a week and that the restaurant menu is for a day. Ask the children what else restaurant menus would have (the price).

● Print the menu and let the children use it as a role-play prop. Model how to phrase requests and orders politely and clearly.

● Help the children to create their own menus. Start with the choices offered, but allow children to introduce their own suggestions too. Where they do this, help them to break words down to spell them and have a dictionary available to check any particularly difficult spellings (Italian and Indian foods are very popular!). This could provide a starting point for a discussion about phonic spelling, with children suggesting which letters could be used to spell the names of foreign dishes and these being checked from various sources, including the internet.

● Help the children to develop a wordbank of dishes to aid them in creating menus.

● More able learners could use the menu to create a shopping list of items that would need to be purchased by the school or restaurant.

Extension

Ask the children to try to find examples of menus. Make a collection of these in the classroom and use them as a starting point for other literacy activities and/or discussions on healthy eating.

The activity could lead to further work on food preferences, with children writing sentences about their favourite and least favourite dishes. They could collect pictures of foods from magazines and bring these to school to illustrate a display of menus.

1: 1: T15: to make simple lists for planning, reminding, and so on

1: 1: W12: to learn new words from reading and shared experiences

side dishes – vegetables and salads – listed under main

menu presented in a table to make it easy to read with different rows for day of the week; main course; dessert; drinks

meat dish listed first

day of the week starts with a capital letter

tells you that these are different options

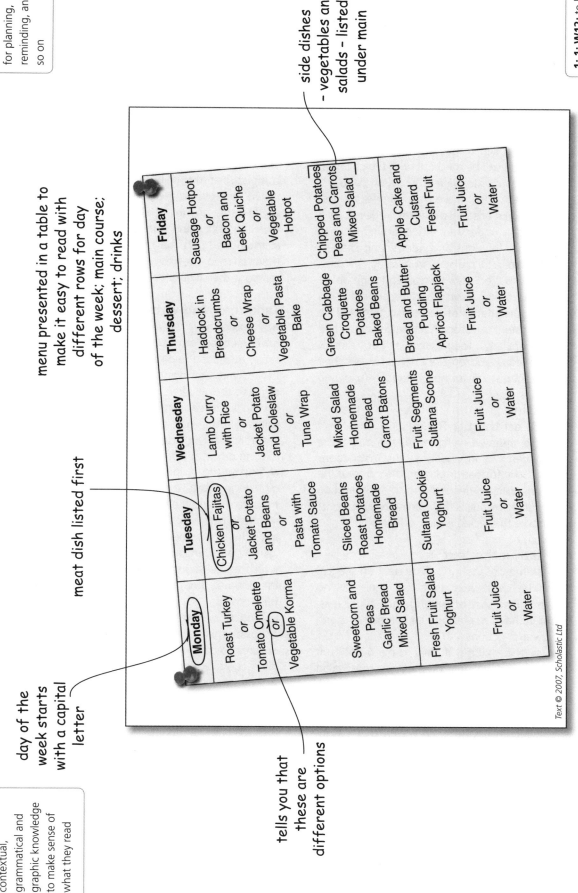

Monday	Tuesday	Wednesday	Thursday	Friday
Roast Turkey or Tomato Omelette or Vegetable Korma	Chicken Fajitas or Jacket Potato and Beans or Pasta with Tomato Sauce	Lamb Curry with Rice or Jacket Potato and Coleslaw or Tuna Wrap	Haddock in Breadcrumbs or Cheese Wrap or Vegetable Pasta Bake	Sausage Hotpot or Bacon and Leek Quiche or Vegetable Hotpot
Sweetcorn and Peas Garlic Bread Mixed Salad	Sliced Beans Roast Potatoes Homemade Bread	Mixed Salad Homemade Bread Carrot Batons	Green Cabbage Croquette Potatoes Baked Beans	Chipped Potatoes Peas and Carrots Mixed Salad
Fresh Fruit Salad Yoghurt	Sultana Cookie Yoghurt	Fruit Segments Sultana Scone	Bread and Butter Pudding Apricot Flapjack	Apple Cake and Custard Fresh Fruit
Fruit Juice or Water	Fruit Juice or Water	Fruit Juice or Water	Fruit Juice or Water	Fruit Juice or Water

Text © 2007, Scholastic Ltd

1: 1: T2: to use phonological, contextual, grammatical and graphic knowledge to make sense of what they read

Recipe: fruit salad
by Claire Head

Background

Following a recipe is a good way to introduce children to procedural texts. This text will allow you to revisit work on lists while developing learning about instructions. Ideally, this recipe for fruit salad will be tried out with the children, and it complements the text 'Fruit' on page 28. Opportunities to make meaningful cross-curricular links arise in the form of developing mathematical understanding: counting, sorting segmenting, fractions and identifying shapes. Learning how to make a fruit salad will also contribute to the 'Eat more fruit and vegetables' QCA Unit 1C in design and technology and work on the theme of healthy eating. Before commencing this lesson check with parents and carers for any food allergies or dietary requirements. Also ensure children wash their hands and put on an apron before following the recipe.

What's on the CD-ROM

The differentiated version of the text is a simplified set of instructions. The instructions are in a table format displaying the name of the fruit, the number needed and the preparation required. This reduces the reading requirements and makes the recipe easier to follow.

Discussing the text

● Ask the class to look at the text (in silence) for 30 seconds and then tell their talking partner what sort of writing they think it is. Establish that it is a recipe that contains lists and a set of instructions.

● Ask the children if they know what fruit salad is. Has anyone ever eaten fruit salad before? If you have worked on the text 'Fruit', recall the children's suggested salads. Explain that there are lots of different ways to make fruit salad, this is just one recipe taken from someone's recipe notebook.

● Identify the title and subheadings and discuss that this text is divided into two lists and one set of instructions. Point out the layout and presentational clues that give this away, such as the long 'columns' of the list and the numbered sequence of sentences in the instructions.

● Read the list of ingredients with the children, pausing to check the quantity listed next to each item. It would be useful if you can prepare a shopping bag containing these ingredients so that you could produce an example of each item as it is read from the list. These fruits could be passed around so that the children could see, smell and touch them. (This multi-sensory experience could then be completed if the children actually made and tasted their own fruit salad.)

● In order to help children to engage fully with the text, hand out sentence strips of the instructions (with the numbers removed) and then, later in the session, ask the children to read out their instruction (with support).

Talk, read and write

● Discuss how the recipe might alternatively have been laid out as labelled diagrams or as a table, and use the differentiated text from the CD-ROM to demonstrate.

● Ask the children to use the differentiated text to tell their partners how to make a fruit salad. Alternatively, they could use toys from the role-play area to perform the actions of making a fruit salad.

● Allow the children to draw and label their own ingredients for a fruit salad. Encourage them to include their favourite fruits.

● Read out the children's sentence strips and ask them to help you to re-order the instructions. Encourage the class to identify which step each instruction is on the numbered list, and ask them to mime the action. (During this process you will need to explain any unfamiliar words.) Begin the re-ordering by choosing the last instruction first to prompt the children to consider whether the order in which instructions are carried out matters.

● Encourage the children to use their sense of taste to describe and identify fruits that you have brought along for the lesson. In small groups, under adequate supervision, give each child a piece of fruit to taste, one at a time. The taster should describe the fruit and then guess what it is. List some of the words used to describe fruit, and see if they could be added to the ingredients to make them clearer.

Extension

Ask children to look at any recipe books at home. Encourage children to bring in handwritten copies of favourite family recipes.

1: 1: **W8:** to read on sight other familiar words

1: 1: **T15:** to make simple lists for planning, reminding, and so on

heading in bold font

sub-headings help to organise the information so instructions are easy to follow

short, simple sentences

Recipe: Fruit Salad

Ingredients
3 bananas
4 apples
5 oranges
1 tin of fruit cocktail
1 tin of pineapple chunks
1 bunch of seedless grapes
1 punnet of strawberries
½ a lemon

Equipment
2 spoons
1 tin opener
1 large bowl
1 small jug
1 peeler
1 sharp knife
1 colander / sieve
1 large chopping board

Text © 2007, Claire Head; photos © 2006, Jupiter Images Corporation

How to make fruit salad

1. Wash the apples, grapes and strawberries.
2. Peel the banana and chop into small chunks. Place in the bowl.
3. Peel the apples and carefully cut into slices. Place in the bowl.
4. Peel the oranges and place segments in the bowl.
5. Pick the grapes and add to the fruit in the bowl.
6. Open the tins of fruit. Drain and save the juice. Pour the fruit into the bowl.
7. Remove the stalks from the strawberries, slice them in half, and place them in the bowl.
8. Pour in some of the saved fruit juice. Squeeze in the juice of half a lemon. Mix everything together gently.
9. Transfer fruit salad into individual dishes and serve. Add one spoonful of ice-cream if desired!

Warning: Be careful when using sharp knives!
Remember to wash your hands before you start preparation.

pictures of ingredients support the text

numbered steps

'bossy verbs' (imperative) used for instructions

subject-specific vocabulary

1: 1: **T13:** to read and follow simple instructions, such as for classroom routines, lists for groups in workbooks

1: 1: **T14:** to write captions for their own work

Light for life

by Gary Gibson

Background

This extract is a good example of how non-fiction books use different presentational devices to communicate information. Photographs and diagrams support the text. The text includes background information, a short explanation and instructions, under subheadings. The instructions for how to grow cress and how to experiment with light for life are made up of a series of sequenced steps, and following these will help children to appreciate the importance of clear instructions. The use of this text could be enhanced by relating it to 'Flowering plants' on page 20 and by engaging in practical activities in science lessons.

What's on the CD-ROM

The CD-ROM contains the instructions for growing cress without the introductory paragraph. This reduces the reading demands providing only required information for actually growing the cress. It can be used to scaffold the core text. The separate steps could be cut up for children to sequence in the correct order to confirm their understanding of the text, with artwork also being correctly matched.

Discussing the text

● Show the children some cress. Ask if anyone has ever tasted cress or grown cress. Look at the colour of the cress – green leaves, white shoots – and talk about how each shoot is rooted in the soil. Ask the children what they think cress needs to live and grow. Scribe their suggestions on the board.

● Tell the children that they are going to be given the opportunity (perhaps in the next science lesson) to grow some cress. Ask the children to work in pairs to list (in words or pictures) the equipment they think will be needed. Invite feedback and add ideas to the words already scribed on the board. Recap by shared reading and agreeing this final class list.

● Explain that although most plants need soil to give them food, cress seeds do not need to be rooted in soil when they are first sown. Explain that you know this fact because you have read some instructions about planting cress that you are now going to share.

● Read the introductory paragraph to the children and explain that they are going to investigate whether cress needs sunlight to live and grow. Ask the children to check on the class list – is *light* one of the things predicted for cress to live and grow?

● Ask the children to identify and label the equipment illustrated in the extract before reading step 1. Explain that the instructions are going to help them conduct the experiment. Read instructions 1 and 2 to the class, pausing to explain unfamiliar words. Next, cover these sentences and ask the children to quickly explain to a friend how to carry out the instructions. Step 3 of this experiment could be shared with the children in a science lesson after the cress has been planted.

Talk, read and write

● During shared or guided writing help the children divide the instructions into smaller steps. Identify and count each sentence in steps 1 and 2 and point out the capital letters at the start of sentences and full stops at the end.

● Make sentence strips so that the children can re-order the instructions. This could be done as an activity in guided groups or as a class 'human sentence' exercise: give individuals words or whole sentences to hold and ask their classmates to put them in the correct order.

● Introduce the use of time connectives to help children order the sentences, for example *first, then, next, finally*. Use these words on large flashcards to prompt children in giving an oral explanation of how to grow cress.

● Ask the children to draw the instructions in the correct sequence and to label each stage. Remind the children to use the class list on the board as a wordbank. Allow them to practise the language of instructional texts by explaining their diagrams to a partner.

● Following the sowing and growing of the cress seeds, read step 3 from the core text and compare the given expectations with the results of the children's experiment. Which seeds have grown the tallest?

Extension

Ask the children to look out for instructions in their homes. Do they have any games at home that have instructions enclosed?

1: 1: **T16**: to write and draw simple instructions and labels for everyday classroom use, such as in role play area, for equipment

additional information is provided by pictures

1: 1: **W12**: to learn new words from reading and shared experiences

1: 1: **S6**: to begin using the term *sentence* to identify sentences in text

non-fiction text contains facts

LIGHT FOR LIFE

Green plants need sunlight to live and grow. They use the light's energy to grow. All animals get their food from plants, either directly or indirectly. Since plants need sunlight to grow, all living things depend on the sun.

GROWING CRESS

1. Put a layer of cotton wool in the bottom of two clean dishes. Dampen with a little water. Sprinkle cress seeds evenly over the cotton wool.

2. Put the dishes on a sunny window sill and cover each dish with a cardboard box. Make a hole in the side of one box and leave for several days. Check daily that the cotton wool is damp.

3. The seeds under the box with no hole have grown straight up looking for light. The cress under the box with the hole has grown toward the light.

Text extract and illustrations from "Science for Fun: Light and Colour" by Gary Gibson © 1994, Aladdin Books Ltd (1994, Watts Books)

title in bold, capital letters for emphasis

introductory sentence provides general information in the present tense

sub-heading in capital letters slightly smaller than title

numbered instructions to help order the information

words (imperative verbs) which give precise instructions

1: 1: **T13**: to read and follow simple instructions, such as for classroom routines, lists for groups in workbooks

1: 1: **T15**: to make simple lists for planning reminding and so on

1: 1: **S5**: to recognise full stops and capital letters when reading, and name them correctly

Plants and seeds — harvesting

by Susan Humphries

Background

This information text about the life cycle of a sunflower plant can be used alongside the text on flowering plants, page 20. It can also be linked to similar work in science and to time in maths. Presenting information in a highly visual format like this makes a text accessible to young children, and reinforces their awareness that information can be presented in a variety of ways.

What's on the CD-ROM

The text on the CD-ROM has the seed-to-seed cycle of a sunflower diagram as on the core text, however the steps are not labelled. The text can be used flexibly to support spoken explanations as children rehearse orally the different stages in the life cycle. Children could also cut out and place the labels in the correct position on the diagram.

Discussing the text

● If possible, have a sunflower and sunflower seeds available to show to the children before they look at the text. You could also show them photographs and pictures of sunflowers. Such as Van Gogh's famous sunflower paintings.

● Begin by looking at the way in which the text is presented (it is predominantly visual, for example) and talk about the fact that it is a page from a book about autumn. Focus on the large picture of the sunflower head and the numbered captions which surround it. Read the captions and talk about the information they provide about the life cycle of the sunflower.

● Read the rest of the text with the children and then ask questions to establish their understanding, for example: *Why do we save some seeds? What do we use sunflower seeds for?*

● Now look more closely at the picture and the seed-to-seed cycle. Explain or elicit from the children that the cycle has similarities with a clock, with the first event at the top just as new hours begin at the top. Help the children to see that the cycle has seven numbered events rather than 12, but that the cycle is presented in clockwise fashion. Talk with the children about clockwise and anti-clockwise and demonstrate their meanings using a clock.

● Highlight some of the key vocabulary (*seed,* *grow, plant, Flower, appear, form, ripen, decays*). Say the phonemes which make up each word, and show how these can be blended together so that we can pronounce them. Establish the meanings of the words and then re-read the captions in the cycle.

● Using a blank version of the diagram, for example from the differentiated text, ask some children to describe the events in the seed-to-seed cycle.

● Talk about the differences in form between the captions on the diagram and the sentences in the main body of the text. Can the children see that the captions are very brief and concise (mainly short phrases of nouns and verbs), while the sentences are longer and more detailed? Ask the children why the captions tend to be brief and discuss this with reference to other captions which they have encountered such as those on signs.

Talk, read and write

● In guided work, focus on the skills required to write captions. Look closely at the captions in the core text, and demonstrate how to turn a caption into a sentence. Support children as they practise creating sentences for some of the stages.

● Provide a picture of a plant (you could use differentiated version of 'Flowering plants', page 20) and ask the children to draw a similar picture of a sunflower. More able learners could add labels which reference the life cycle text or which show the different parts of a sunflower.

● Use some of the key topic words from the text and the children's growing understanding of the seed-to-seed cycle to help them to write sentences of their own about plant growth.

Extension

Ask children to bring examples of different seeds to school so that a collection and display can be made. Sow some of the seeds so that children can monitor their growth and see how the cycle works in real life. Encourage children to note what they see periodically. Take digital photographs to record the progress of the seeds' growth and store these on the computer together with notes made by the children.

technical words linked to topic

captions not written in full sentences

large clear typeface used for captions to make them stand out

Plants and seeds

HARVESTING

We always save some seeds from the harvested crop for future planting. We can then grow the same crop next year.

1. Seed

2. Seed begins to grow

3. Plant grows

4. Flower appears

5. Seeds begin to form

6. Seeds ripen

7. Plant decays

This is the seed-to-seed cycle of a sunflower.

A mature sunflower head has a beautiful pattern of seeds in the centre. If you store some ripe seeds you can plant them in the spring or give them to birds in the winter. We harvest sunflowers for the oil in their seeds.

[Text extract and illustrations from "Autumn" by Susan Humphries © 1986, Macdonald & Co (Publishers) Ltd; photo © Carlos Zaragoza]

number to show the order of the stages

arrows show that the steps are set out in clockwise direction

each step is illustrated by a clear diagram which provides additional information

caption to explain entire diagram

Create an autumn leaves display

by Claire Head

Background

This text of suggestions for a class display using autumn leaves is presented in the form of a poster. It draws on a variety of presentation and layout devices, including detailed diagrams and numbered lists, which can be considered alongside looking at typical language features. You will be able to make cross-curricular links to art and design and topic work connected with autumn, plants and trees, and woodland creatures. The poster could also be used in conjunction with the earlier text 'Leaves' on page 18 and the non-chronological report 'Owls' on page 102.

What's on the CD-ROM

The differentiated text included on the CD-ROM is a set of instructions for making a blackbird from sycamore leaves, relating to the feathery owl that can be created from the core text. In following these instructions, children will build on skills they will have acquired from studying the core text and in using other instructions. Alternatively, the steps could be cut out and given to the children to re-order, to allow them to practise sequencing skills. Or the illustrations could be cut out and given to children with the instruction to match the illustration to its text.

Discussing the text

● Look at the poster and ask the children to tell you what sort of information it is presenting. Read the title and point out some of the features of non-fiction texts, for example the subheadings in bold, the boxes that have been used to pick out the diagrams, the sentences that are numbered – typical of a set of instructions.

● Read the list of resources and explain that these have been provided to help the reader prepare the equipment needed to make the display. Tell the children that they are going to work together to make this display and might think of more resources to add to this list.

● Next, ask the children to look carefully at the rest of the poster and tell you how many steps they need to follow to make a *printed leaves* picture. (4.) Read these instructions to the children and pause to talk about how the pictures help us to understand the process.

● Highlight some of the features of instructional texts, such as the numbered stages, use of simple, clear sentences, and the way in which the text addresses the reader directly. Compare the two sets of instructions for *Printed Leaves and A Feathery Owl* and show how *First, Then, Next* and *Finally* work in the same way as numbers. To test this, swap *1* for *First*, *2* for *Then* and so on between the two sections.

● To develop this, model how to use time connectives to order instructions. (You could use the differentiated text from the CD-ROM) and then ask the children to practise using these in simple sentences, perhaps about getting ready for school or playing a game.

● Summarise what has been learned so far by reminding the children that good instructions explain: *what* is to be done, *how* it is to be done, and *why* you might like to do this.

● Focus on the suggestion for making a picture of a feathery owl. Ask the children to think of ways of using the technique to create feathers for another bird. What birds could they create? What colours would they need?

Talk, read and write

● Print the instructions for the blackbird from the CD-ROM, and provide the necessary resources for children to follow the instructions. More confident children could improvise on the idea, and create other bird pictures.

● Once the children have created their pictures, encourage them to tell a friend how they made their bird. Remind them to use time connectives, and to sequence their explanation clearly. Some children might be able now to add captions to their paintings which describe how they made them.

● To further reinforce the skills of reading and writing instructions in order, the blackbird text could be cut up into separate steps for children to re-order.

Extension

Take the class on a leaf hunt. Take digital photographs of the children collecting leaves and drawing pictures of nearby trees. (Ensure you get parents' or carers' permission before taking photographs.) Use these as part of a display and as the basis of a matching game (naming the trees and their leaves).

signs

1: 1: T14: to write captions for their own work

1: 1: W8: to read on sight other familiar words

four numbered steps

addresses the reader directly

time connectives

How to Create an Autumn Leaves Display

RESOURCES

You will need:
A selection of different leaves
Some paint – (red, yellow, brown, green and black)
Paint brushes
– (different sizes)
Glue
Twigs
A pencil
Paper
Some felt-tips

PRINTED LEAVES
Follow four easy steps to create an amazing autumn picture.

1. Choose a leaf and select a paint colour.
2. Paint one side of the leaf and then press it down on your sheet of paper.
3. Peel the leaf away carefully. You will see a leaf print left behind.
4. Repeat this action using different leaves and choosing different paint colours.

A FEATHERY OWL
Use the same printing technique to create a fantastic feathery owl picture.

What to do:
First draw the owl's head, eyes and beak at the top of your paper.
Then use small leaves to print the feathers on the owl's body.
Next give your owl two printed feet.
Finally fix a twig along the bottom of your picture so your owl has something to perch on.

Now you are ready to display all your hard work!

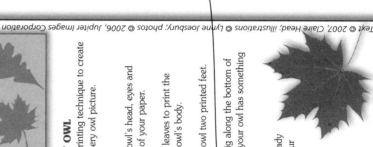

title is in large, coloured outline font

sub-headings in bold capital letters

addresses the reader

illustrations support the written instructions

1: 1: T13: to read and follow simple instructions

1: 1: S4: to write captions and simple sentences

1: 1: T16: to write and draw simple instructions

Model toys

by Scholastic Ltd

Background
This text is from a simple non-fiction book about toys. The page has a title, *Model toys*, two large pictures which can promote discussion and writing, and simple one-line sentences with repeated vocabulary. This text could be used as an introduction to the topic of toys, and can be linked to the following two texts ('Toys then and now' and 'My beautiful doll') and work in history.

What's on the CD-ROM
The differentiated text on the CD-ROM uses two sets of questions to encourage children to look more closely at a text. Ideally, these questions should be used as prompts for paired discussion. Using the *Words which might help you* box as a prompt, children can make up (and possibly write down) their own questions.

Discussing the text
● Show the children the text, but cover the title. After looking at the pictures and some of the sentences, ask the children to suggest what the title might be. Reveal the title and then ask the children what they notice about the way in which it is printed. Why do they think it is in bold type? Why is the font larger than for the rest of the text? Talk about titles and show some other examples to illustrate that they are usually presented in a way which makes them stand out from other text. What else do the children notice about the layout? (They might talk about the large photographs and short sentences.)

● Ask the children to decide whether this text is taken from a story book or a book which gives information. Introduce or revise the terms *fiction* and *non-fiction*, and discuss which of the above features are usually found in a non-fiction book. Encourage the children to think about the different purposes of both kinds of book. Ask: *What does a fiction book do? What does a non-fiction book do? Who this book might be written for?*

● Read the text in full with the children and encourage them to talk about their own experiences of model toys. The text claims that the models look real. Do they agree?

● Focus on the words *model* and *real* and draw attention to their language features.

Segment the words and talk about other words which have some similar sounds. For example, for *model*: god, rod, cod, pod and *label, parcel*; and for *real*: *heal, seal, steal* and *deal*.

Talk, read and write
● Adapt the questions in the differentiated text to encourage the children to look more closely at the core text. See if they can answer the questions from the information given.

● Model how to write the answers to the questions, prompting the children to remind you where to place capital letters and full stops. Then ask the children to make up some questions of their own about the text, and write these on the board with their help. Draw their attention to the use of question marks.

● Go on to ask questions which require interpretation as well as observation. For example: *Do you think the picture shows a modern garage or one from many years ago?*

● Highlight particularly useful topic words in the text and add to the list by discussing what can be seen in the pictures. Read through the list with the children. Establish how the words should be pronounced and segment them into phonemes. Look for opportunities to help children to extrapolate from what they learn about the words in the lists to develop their ability to apply their growing phonic knowledge to other words. For example, when looking at the word *sheep* talk about other words which begin with 'sh', and others which have the 'e' sound made by 'ee', such as *keep, deep* and *peep*. When looking at the word *cows* talk about other words with an 'ow' sound made with 'ow', such as *now* and *how*.

Extension
Ask children to bring model toys from home, and make a display of these accompanied by short pieces of writing by the children about the age of the models and any interesting facts about them.

1: 2: T24: to write simple questions, such as as part of interactive display

use of photographs typical of non-fiction texts. Reinforces understanding that these are real objects.

rhyming words: heal, seal, steal and deal.

1: 2: W3: to discriminate, read and spell words with initial consonant clusters, such as 'bl', 'cr', 'tr', 'str' – Appendix List 3

Model toys

Some toys are models of things.
This is a model garage.
It has a car wash and space for cars to park.

Models like like real things.
Can you see what this is a model of?
It is a model farm.

Text © 2007, Scholastic Ltd; photos courtesy of Heritage Play Sets, www.heritageplaysets.com

heading in large, bold font.

create rhyming string with similar words, e.g. God, rod, cod, pod and label, parcel

layout of page with illustrations supported by text makes this easy for young readers to follow.

information text written in the present tense. Simple, clear sentences.

1: 2: T17: to use terms 'fiction' and 'non-fiction', noting some of their differing features, such as layout, titles, contents page, use of pictures, labelled diagrams

1: 2: S7: to use capital letters for the personal pronoun 'I', for names and for the start of a sentence

Toys then and now

by David Waugh

Background

The text comprises captioned pictures of toys past and present, which can be used as a basis for discussing similarities and differences between today's toys, and toys from the past. If possible, arrange a collection of toys similar to those in the text available for children to look at. The text can be linked to other texts in this term, particularly 'My beautiful doll', page 48, 'Model toys', page 44, as well as to enquiry work in history.

What's on the CD-ROM

The differentiated text on the CD-ROM includes images of a selection of different toys, some from the past, and some more contemporary. You may wish to add other toys to the text, especially those which are very popular at Christmas time. Children can use the questions given on the sheet to scaffold conversations about a wide variety of toys. More able learners could write simple captions which describe the toys, and classify them as *then* or *now*.

Discussing the text

● Begin by asking the children about their favourite toys. Which toys did they receive as presents recently? What do they particularly like about the toys? Do they have any toys which their grandparents/parents/older siblings say that they had too when they were children?

● Display the text, but hide the captions next to the illustrations. Begin by looking at the pictures one by one. Ask the children if they know the names of the toys. Check their predictions by uncovering and reading the captions. Look for the key words which say what the toy is called.

● Talk about each of the toys and explain how some of the less familiar ones were used. If possible, show the children some of the toys and let them try them out. Spend some time discussing the questions that are raised in the captions.

● Next, ask the children which of the toys they think were played with before they were born. Talk about the words *then* and *now* and ask the children to suggest some toys from the text which are still played with now and some which are no longer popular, such as the *jack-in-the-box*, which might therefore be labelled *then*.

● Look at the spellings of some of the words and focus upon the initial consonant cluster 'tr' in *tricycle* and *trike*. Ask the children if they can think of any other words which begin with 'tr' (for example *truck* from the differentiated text). Then talk about the prefix 'tri', which means three. Relate this to the three wheels on the tricycle. Do the children know another word with this prefix which has three of something (for example, *triangle*, *tripod*, *triple*)? Now look at the 'ck' sound in *rocket*, *jack* (and *truck*) and explain that this 'k' sound never occurs at the beginnings of words, but can often be found at the end or in the middle. Look at some other words which have 'ck' in them, such as *luck*, *tick*, *back*, *brick* and *trick*.

Talk, read and write

● Discuss again *then* and *now* and look at the differentiated text with the children. Ask the children to name and describe the toys to each other and then to you. Ask questions about the toys in addition to those on the sheet, for example: *How do you think children played with them? Which had moving parts? Which have you played with?*

● Demonstrate how to write a simple caption, using the questions to scaffold your writing. Segment and blend individual words as you write them, especially those that reinforce spelling patterns addressed during the whole-class session (such as *rocking horse*).

● Work with less able writers to add labels to the pictures. Encourage them to add a picture of their favourite toy and write a simple sentence about it.

Extension

Encourage children to find out more about the toys their parents or grandparents played with. If possible, ask them to bring some examples to school which could form part of a display of toys. Look at the website for the V&A Museum of Childhood (www.vam.ac.uk/moc), which has lots of information about toys through the ages.

TOYS THEN AND NOW

1: 2: T23: to produce extended captions

use of questions to encourage investigation and exploration

1: 2: W10: to learn new words from reading and shared experiences

compare this model with other model toys available

Text © 2007, David Waugh; photos © 2006, Jupiter Images Corporation

Look carefully at these pictures of toys. Are they like the toys you play with? How are they different?

The yo-yo was invented thousands of years ago. The first yo-yos were made out of stone. Later, people carved yo-yos out of wood. What are today's yo-yos made out of?

The first tricycles were built over 160 years ago, long before cars were invented. They were used by adults as a way of getting around – and they were much bigger than the trike you can see here. Who are trikes made for today?

This is a jack-in-the-box. If you turn the handle on the side, it plays a tune. At the end of the tune, the lid opens and a small toy on springs pops out. Why do you think it is called a jack-in-the-box?

People have always made models of everyday things for children to play with. Is this model rocket a modern toy, or is it a toy from the past? How do you know?

Teddy bears come in all sorts of colours, shapes and sizes. How old is this bear? The first teddy bears were made over 100 years ago.

1: 2: T22: to write labels for drawings and diagrams

introduces the topic; addresses the reader directly

this is oldest of the toys described here

consonant cluster

ensure children make the connection between 'trike' and 'tricycle'. Children may be intrigued to find out that people rode bikes and trikes because cars had not been invented

named after American president Theodore Roosevelt who, on a hunting trip in 1902, refused to shoot a bear that had been caught and tied up

1: 2: W7: to recognise the critical features of words

My beautiful doll

by Scholastic Ltd

Background

This text consists of a recount about a favourite toy. It was written by a girl who wanted to share her memories about a special doll her grandmother gave her when she was young. The doll is porcelain and provides a good oppotunity to discuss how toys have changed . This text is best used in conjunction with the two previous extracts in this term.

What's on the CD-ROM

A writing frame has been created here to encourage children to write their own descriptions of favourite toys. This could be demonstrated initially by you describing your favourite childhood toy. More able writers could work independently, while less able learners may need additional support in the form of sentence starters for each section.

Discussing the text

● If this is the first text about toys you are using, ask the children to think, pair and share with their partners about a favourite toy. Encourage the children to explain why that particular toy is special to them.

● Tell the children that the text they are going to read is all about a special toy. The text descibes a doll given to a girl by her grandmother when she was younger and she still has it to this day.

● Read the text together before beginning to focus in detail on sections.

● Re-read and discuss the detailed description of the doll. Ask: *Why was a detailed description included? Would you know what the doll looked like without it?* Elicit that it is because there is no picture to refer to. Ask the children to close their eyes and imagine the doll to create their own picture.

● Discuss the different materials used to make and descibe the doll: *porcelain, cardboard, silk, linen.* Ask the children if they know what these materials are. If possible have some examples to show the children. Talk to them about their toys. Ask questions such as: *Are your toys made from these materials too? What other materials are toys made from?*

● Look at the final sentence. Ask the children why they think the doll is *faded* and *scratched* now. How old do they think the girl is now?

Why? How old do they think the doll is? Encourage the children to use clues from the text to answer these questions for example: *When I was **six**, my Grandma gave me an old **doll of hers** for Christmas.* Do the children think that the doll still sounds beautiful? Why does it still seem beautiful to the girl?

Talk, read and write

● Re-read the desciption of the doll and remind the children what the different materials look like, and if possible feel like. Ask the children to draw and label the doll. Ideally you could show the children a similar doll, visit a toy museum or use reference books to help the children to continue this research. Demonstrate how to create a fuller caption for the illustration,.

● Invite the children to bring in their favourite toy and, after some oral rehearsal, describe it, and write about why it is special. Encourage children to begin some sentences with the capitalised personal pronoun 'I' and to use capital letters for names, for example *I like my teddy. He is called Fred...* Take digital photographs of the toys and encourage the children to write captions to accompany the photographs on a display.

● In guided writing help children to write clues for their special toys, along with 'What am I?' captions.

Extension

Ask children to talk to members of their family about favourite toys that they remember playing with. Remind children to ask why the toys were special to their owners.

With parents' or carers' permission children could be encouraged to bring in unwanted toys to donate to a children's charity.

1: 2: T23: to produce extended captions

detailed description given as photo isn't available

when the doll was made

concluding statement reflects author's point of view

1: 2: S7: to use capital letters for 'I', for names and for the start of a sentence

My beautiful doll

When I was six, my Grandma gave me an old doll of hers for Christmas. I still have her today. Her head, legs and arms are made of painted porcelain, and her body is made of cardboard. Her shoes are black, shiny paint. She is dressed in a silk bonnet tied under the chin. Her skirt is made of linen, trimmed with lace and underneath she wears a cream-coloured combination. Her date of birth is written on the back of her neck. I hardly dared to play with her in case I broke her. I wouldn't let anyone else pick her up because she was too special. Her clothes are faded now and some of her painting is scratched but she is still beautiful to me.

Text © 2007, Scholastic Ltd; photo © 2006, Jupiter Images Corporation

1: 2: T22: to write labels for drawing and diagrams

opening sentence tells the reader when this event took place

1st person pronouns used for personal recount

old-fashioned type of underwear

1: 2: T25: to assemble information from own experience

Touch

edited by Mandy Suhr

Background

This extract from *The Senses – Touch* is a simple, factual text which begins to explain how we use our sense of touch to feel things. The brief report, accompanied by a labelled diagram and cartoon illustrations, will provide a good starting point for children's work on the senses. It links to the extract 'Make a string telephone' in Term 3, page 78, and to science work on 'Ourselves' and 'Sorting and using materials'.

What's on the CD-ROM

The differentiated text provided on the CD-ROM is based around an investigative activity which requires children to draw around their hands and to touch, describe and name five different textures in the classroom. This will help children to experience, first-hand, the sensations described in the core text.

Discussing the text

● Explain to the children that this text will help them find out about one of their senses. Ask the children to talk about what the word *sense* refers to and whether they can list the five senses and show which parts of the body are used by which sense. They may need some clues so you could write the initial letters of each sense word on the board.
● Tell the children that you are going to read the first sentence of this text and they should listen carefully and put their hands up as soon as they have worked out which sense this text is giving information about (and how they can tell).
● Talk about the word *texture*. If possible, relate to work in science about materials and their properties. Use examples around the classroom to illustrate this word, for example *soft* cushions, *smooth* table tops, the *rough* sole on a shoe.
● Read the next sentence and give the children a chance to look at the humorous illustration which accompanies it. Provide other real life examples of objects which have a different texture on the outside from that on the inside, such as an orange, a coconut, a chocolate bar. Help the children to appreciate that even though this text has cartoon drawings it is still a non-fiction text.

● Read the remainder of the text and focus on the labelled diagram that illustrates the *touch detectors*. Explain that this picture is an example of how the skin might look close-up through a microscope. Ask the children to help you read the labels and then talk about which parts of the skin shown are on the outside and which are on the inside. Ask the children to brush their hands gently along their forearms to feel the soft hairs that help to detect touch. What do the children think *detect* means?

Talk, read and write

● Create a cloze procedure activity from the text. Delete words that are central to meaning in each sentence, for example *feels* and *texture*, or focus on sight vocabulary, such as *way*, can, and *very*. Model the exercise during guided group work and then provide opportunities for children to work in pairs to complete the sentences with missing words.
● During shared or guided reading ask the children to spot the initial consonant blends in the text: *skin, small, special, strong*. Practise sounding out and stretching these words to help the children count the phonemes. Use the words *skin* and *small* as the starting point for onset and rime activities. Then identify consonant digraphs (*things, touch*) and talk about the way that together these letters make a new sound of their own.
● Identify the compound words in the text: *inside* and *outside*. Ask the children if they can spot the parts of these words that are the same and if they can see the two words within one. Then ask the children to find one more word in the text that is made up of two words that can be used separately (*something*).
● Work with small groups to identify mystery objects in a feely bag. Encourage the children to describe how each object feels and, after some oral rehearsal, to write simple clues for one of the objects.

Extension

Ask children to be touch detectives and to use their touch detectors to detect three different textures in their homes. Children can report back with oral descriptions in a subsequent lesson.

1: 2: T25: to assemble information from own experience

simple present tense used for report

labelled diagram supports the text

technical vocabulary linked with scientific investigation

1: 2: W7: to recognise the critical features of words

Text extract and illustrations from "The Senses – Touch" edited by Mandy Suhr © 1993, Wayland (Publishers) Limited

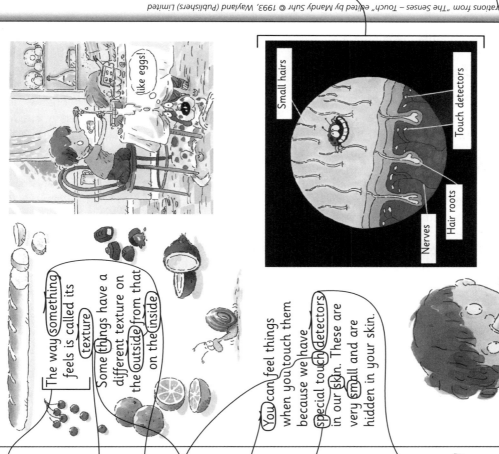

TOUCH

(like eggs!)

The way something feels is called its texture

Some things have a different texture on the outside from that on the inside

You can feel things when you touch them because we have special touch detectors in our skin. These are very small and are hidden in your skin.

Small hairs

Touch detectors

Nerves

Hair roots

To see the touch detectors you need a very strong microscope.

explanation and definition of topic given in first sentence

key word

compound words

consonant digraph

addresses the reader directly

initial consonant blends

technical vocabulary, requires explanation which is given in following sentence

1: 2: T17: to use terms 'fiction' and 'non-fiction', noting some of their differing features

1: 2: W3: to discriminate, read and spell words with initial consonant clusters, such as 'bl', 'cr', 'tr', 'str'; to blend phonemes in words with clusters for reading; to segment clusters into phonemes for spelling

Waste

by Terry Jennings

Background

This simple information text describes what happens to our domestic and municipal waste and what sort of waste can be recycled. This extract could act as the springboard for a project on recycling which might involve finding out what happens to the school's rubbish. It links to the QCA science Unit 1C 'Sorting and using materials', which requires children to identify and classify materials and their properties. This theme is also explored in two other extracts in this term: 'Wrapping it up' on page 104 and 'What is a bike made of?' on page 106.

What's on the CD-ROM

The differentiated text is entitled: *Reduce, reuse and recycle*. This text develops ideas from the core text and aims to help children to learn about the different ways that 'rubbish' can be sorted and treated to help the environment. Children can use the sheet to support paired discussion of the topic. The items of rubbish listed on the sheet can be cut out and placed in the appropriate category.

Discussing the text

● If possible, prepare for the lesson by collecting several days' worth of rubbish, including what remains of the day's packed lunches. (Be selective about what you save and ensure that cartons and bottles have been washed out and avoid rotting food!) Ask the children to sit in a circle on the carpet. Place a sheet of plastic on the floor in the centre and empty the rubbish onto the mat.

● Tell the children that they are going to help you to sort the rubbish, but first you are going to learn more about waste. Read the title of the extract and talk about the meaning. Relate it to the words *rubbish* and *refuse*.

● Point out and read the two subheadings in bold. Ask the children if they know what happens to the rubbish after it has been placed in the bin at home and then read *Getting rid of waste*.

● Put on a pair of protective gloves and explain to the children that this is a health and safety precaution. The children do not need to touch the rubbish.

● Place four large hoops on the carpet and explain that you are going to use these to help sort your rubbish. Label the hoops: *plastic, paper, metal* and *glass*. As you select each item from the rubbish pile ask the children to say what sort of material it is made of and what food type it used to contain, for example *plastic – yoghurt*. After sorting the rubbish, talk about which set contains the most items.

● Next, read the explanation of recycling and ask if anyone has heard of this word before. Highlight the materials that can be recycled according to the text (*paper, glass, metals*). Draw a connecting line to objects in the text that are made of these materials: *bottles, cans* and *newspapers*. Look at your sets of rubbish again and talk about which of these can be recycled.

● Now look at the layout of the text, focusing on the use of a main heading and subheadings to organise the information. Examine the photographs and discuss how they provide additional details. Ask the children to suggest possible captions or labels, and model adding them to the text.

Talk, read and write

● Consider the amount of rubbish you have collected and explain how important it is to cut down the amount of rubbish we produce. Introduce the three Rs: reduce, reuse and recycle. Ask the children to think about how they could reuse some of the items in the circles instead of throwing them away. For example, the yoghurt pot could be used as a paint pot or a plant pot. Use the differentiated version of the text to help the children to identify and group different materials.

● Ask the children to design posters to be placed around the school with captions and labels advertising the three Rs.

● Create a cloze version of the text by masking high frequency words, such as *Some, can* and *You*, and/or key topic words, such as *waste, paper, recycling*.

Extension

Ask children to talk to their families about things that could be recycled at home.

Set up recycling bins in the classroom, and create labels for each bin.

1: 2: T23: to produce extended captions

1: 2: W10: to learn new words from reading and shared experiences

1: 2: W5: to read on sight other familiar words

connection between objects and the type of material they are made of

technical vocabulary

simple sentences

general opening statement introduces topic

main heading in large, bold letters

high frequency words

'ed' ending

Waste

People in villages, towns , and cities throw away lots of waste.

Recycling

Waste can be sorted. The old paper, glass, and metals are used to make new paper, glass and metals. This is called recycling.

There may be special recycling bins where you live. You can leave bottles, cans and newspapers to be collected for recycling.

Getting rid of waste

Most waste is taken away in special lorries. Some waste is tipped into big holes in the ground. Some waste is burned.

Text extract from "Exploring where you live" by Terry Jennings © 1995, Terry Jennings (1995; Oxford University Press); photos: recycle centre © Vicky S, rubbish bins © Denise Hunter

uses photographs to provide more information

sub-headings in smaller bold font

1: 2: T22: to write labels for drawings and diagrams

1: 2: W4: to read on sight high frequency words

A–Z

by Scholastic Children's Books

Background

Many children are thrilled by the mysterious and supernatural, particularly anything ghoulish! This activity focuses on the back cover of a 'ghostly' reference book for children. Used alongside some of the other texts in Term 2 (for example, 'Touch', page 50 and 'Waste', page 52) it will extend children's awareness of features of non-fiction books. Arrange for a varied selection of non-fiction books to be available during the lesson so that children can make comparisons between the layout and features of different book covers.

What's on the CD-ROM

The differentiated text provided on the CD-ROM takes the form of a template so that children can take part in a shared writing activity to produce a book cover of their own. You may wish to link this activity to some of the other topics covered in this resource, such as toys, pets or homes.

Discussing the text

● Show the children the cover of the book and ask them to tell you the title. What do they think of it? Does it make them want to take a look inside the book? What do they think they will find? Ask the children to predict what kind of book this is, and whether they are familiar with any other A–Z books (such as dictionaries, or alphabetically organised information books). Establish whether this is likely to be a story book or a book which gives information. The author's name does not appear, but is on the spine (not reproduced), and the illustrator's name is on the back cover.

● Discuss the choice of font for the title, and how this supports the theme and tone of the book. Note the alphabetical border around the cover, and the small illustrations.

● Now point out the features of a typical back cover: blurb, publisher's name, ISBN and bar code, price and the web address. Discuss the purpose of this information.

● Read the blurb to the children. Discuss whether the blurb confirms their predictions about the likely content of the book. Although this is a non-fiction title, the book includes a few 'tales', some of which are likely to be fictional stories. Encourage the children to talk about whether the blurb makes them want to read the book.

● Re-read the blurb to the children, and ask them to put up their hands every time there are two or more words next to or very near each other which start with the same letter. This blurb makes considerable use of alliteration to make it more engaging. (*Haunted houseful; spooky surprises; fearsome facts.*)

Talk, read and write

● Look at the writing frame on the CD-ROM and explain to the children that they are going to help you to produce a cover for a book about one of the themes you have been discussing in class recently (such as homes, pets or toys). Read through the list of information required for each part of the cover and ask the children to suggest what might be written in each place. Revise how to spell certain words by segmenting them into phonemes.

● Show the children other examples of book covers so that they can see the kind of information which tends to be provided and the ways in which it can be set out.

● Allow more able learners to create their own book cover, some at the computer if possible. Less able learners could use the wording you have created, and focus on the design of the cover, thinking about the style of lettering, illustrations and colour to make the cover as appealing as possible.

Extension

With the class, go on to make a book to go with the cover produced. Show the children a contents page to give them an idea of what such a book might contain and ask children to find out about different sub-topics at home and by using books at school.

Make a display of non-fiction books centered around a Big Book which has different features of the cover labelled.

1: 2: W10: to learn new words from reading and shared experiences

wacky typeface supports theme of the book

first sentence of blurb encourages you to read the book by saying that you 'need' it

Back cover of "The A–Z of ghosts, skeletons and other haunting horrors" by Tracey Turner, illustrated by Kate Sheppard; cover © 2004, Scholastic Children's Books

A-Z

Whether you're completely fearless or a complete scaredy-cat, you need this book. Open it and discover a haunted houseful of spooky surprises packed with fearsome facts, quizzes, stories, games and other things to do.

Find out:

☆ how to trick or treat, carve a pumpkin and other scary essentials

☆ what to do if you meet a werewolf

☆ some terrifying tales you might believe... and a few you certainly won't.

Read on and dig up a host of horribly haunting horrors – from A to Z.

Illustrated by Kate Sheppard

A-Z
NON-FICTION
UK **£3.99**
SCHOLASTIC
ZONE www.scholastic.co.uk/zone

ISBN 0-439-96326-5
9 780439 963268

A-Z suggests that the information might be arranged alphabetically; it's comprehensive

blurb addresses the reader directly to encourage them to read the book

tells you that the book is a mixture of fiction and non-fiction

illustrations of bats reinforce theme

– reinforces A-Z reference theme of title

name of publisher

1: 2: T19: to predict what a given book might be about from a brief look at both front and back covers

1: 2: T17: to use terms 'fiction' and 'non-fiction', noting some of their differing features

Index

by Judy Bastyra

Background

This index is for a book about food. The layout is very simple and clear, as this may be the first time children have encountered text in this format. Most of the vocabulary should be familiar to the children, although they may not recognise the words in written form. The index can be looked at in conjunction with other books which have indexes, and should provide an opportunity to discuss types of text which are a feature of non-fiction but not fiction. The text can be linked to 'Fruit', page 20, and 'Flowering plants', page 28, and should provide opportunities for vocabulary building. It also ties in with 'How does a flower grow?' on page 58 and 'Contents and index', page 60.

What's on the CD-ROM

The differentiated version of the text is a randomly ordered list of food items. These can be cut out and arranged in alphabetical order. They could also be sorted in other ways, for example according to different types of food or to focus on different word structures such as CVC words, words with initial consonant clusters or final consonant clusters.

Discussing the text

● Show the children the index and ask if they know what it is and where it might be found. Read the words to them and then with them and discuss how the index is set out, ensuring that the children notice that it comprises both words and numbers. Talk about how an index can help us to locate information in a book. Show the children a simple book (preferably a Big Book), which has an index and ask them to help you to find information on some of the listed items.

● Now focus on the page references for *butter*, *cheese*, *milk* and *yoghurt*, and consider why they share a common page number. Ask the children to spot any other words which share a page reference.

● Pick out certain words in the index and ask the children to identify those which are plurals. Prompt by asking questions such as: *Does the book tell us about only one kind of animal/plant/vegetable? What letter tells us that there is more than one?*

● Discuss plurals further in the context of things which can be seen around the classroom. Some of the plurals the children mention might be irregular (*children*, for example), but at this stage keep the focus on those which are made by adding 's' or 'es'.

● Look at some of the words closely as they are read aloud and, with the children's help, identify those which have initial or final consonant clusters, for example *grains*. Then ask them to think of other words with similar clusters: *grin, grow, grab*.

Talk, read and write

● Re-read the list with the children. Talk about the spellings and show how the words can be segmented into phonemes to help us to say them.

● Ask the children to think of some other items which might appear in a book about food and write these on the board. Add the items to the index, asking the children to suggest where they should be placed in alphabetical order.

● Ask pairs or small groups to create their own indexes about food, either for an imaginary book or for books which you provide from the library.

● Work with children who need more support to talk more about alphabetical order and to guide them as they read the list of foods on the differentiated text and put them into alphabetical order. Encourage them to do this in an organised way, beginning by looking for words which begin with 'a', then 'b' and so on, and writing these down in lists before organising them further by referring to second and third letters for those which begin with the same letters. As four words begin with 'c', it would be best to leave organising these words until last.

Extension

Ask children to find other examples of indexes in the class or school library and/or at home and to bring these to the next lesson to share with the class. These might include some which have more than one column, which could lead to a discussion about different layouts. Catalogues for shopping are of particular interest to children and can be linked to work on toys.

50 Shared texts Non-fiction ● Year 1

1: 2: W8: to investigate and learn spellings of words with 's' for plurals

where there are multiple references, pages listed in numerical order

simple plural 's'

note final consonant cluster

Index

animals 2, 4, 5, 6, 11
butter 6
cheese 6
eggs 6
energy 2, 8
fish 5, 6
fruit 4, 8, 14
grains 4, 5, 10, 11
meat 2, 5, 6
milk 6, 8
plants 2
salad vegetables 15
seeds 14
shopping 18, 19
vegetables 4, 5, 15
yoghurt 6, 8

Index from "Get Set Go! Vegetables" by Judy Bastyra © 1994, Judy Bastyra (1994, Franklin Watts); photos: peppers and tomatoes © Andre Veron, strawberries © Katryn McCallum

note the common page reference (6) which suggests that these foods would be found in a 'dairy' section

note initial consonant cluster

alphabetical ordering by second letter

1: 2: T21: to understand the purpose of contents pages and indexes and to begin to locate information by page numbers and words by initial letter

1: 2: W3: to discriminate, read and spell words with initial consonant clusters, such as 'bl', 'cr', 'tr', 'str'

How does a flower grow?

by Scholastic Ltd

Background

This contents page from *How does a flower grow?* includes features often found on a title page, such as the title and the names of the author, designer, illustrator and series editor. Ideally, children will have access to collections of books about flowers to make comparisons between different front pages and contents pages and how they link to the book content. Note that in this example, the page given for each section is the one on which the section starts. Some contents pages in books for young children show the range of pages. You might need to discuss different ways of presenting the page numbers with children, especially if they have already seen different ways of setting them out. The text can be linked to 'Flowering plants' on page 20.

What's on the CD-ROM

This text has a simplified contents text with fewer items, which have been listed in the wrong order. It can be developed by adding further sections with appropriate page numbers. You can discuss possible section titles with children and add these to the list, practising alphabetical order and number order.

Discussing the text

● Display the text and ask if anyone can explain what a contents page is and what the numbers signify. Compare the page with other examples from books in the classroom. Discuss why a contents page is useful in a non-fiction book.

● Look at the layout of the text more closely and then talk briefly about the jobs done by the author, illustrator, designer and series editor. Show the children some other books which provide similar information. Ask the children why they think Bill Bruce's name comes first and why he is the only person whose role is not stated. (He is the author.)

● Read through the list of sections and then ask the children to read them with you. Discuss any unfamiliar words and talk about the way in which the sections listed have brief titles intended to let the reader know what he or she can expect to find.

● Explain that the numbers indicate the page

on which each of the sections begins. Provide the children with books containing similar contents pages for the children to explain.

● Look at some of the words in the text which begin with consonant clusters, for example *flowers, closer, Growing* and *plant*. Practise the pronunciation of these words and show the children how they can be segmented to help us to read them, for example *fl-ow-er-s, gr-ow, pl-a-nt*.

Talk, read and write

● Check children's understanding of how a contents page works by asking questions about locating information, for example *Which page would I go to if I wanted to read about seeds? What information would I find on page 22?* Then allow the children to take it in turn to make up similar questions of their own.

● Look at the differentiated text with some children and read the section headings with them. Explain that this is a first draft of a book that the publishers are still working on, and some of the sections are out of order. Their role is to be the editor and put the sections in the right order. Help them to think of further titles for sections on flowers and talk about how the sections should be arranged correctly in number order, you could also discuss alphabetical order. Guide them as they write additional section headings. If they or you run out of ideas, refer to some of the books which you collected or to relevant websites.

Extension

Encourage children to look at lots of examples of contents pages and to discuss layout and included features with adults and other pupils. Make a display of copies of contents pages and place the books alongside so that children can use the books in conjunction with the display.

Make a class book to go with a topic the children are studying in another area of the curriculum and compile a contents page for placing at the front.

1: 2: W3: to discriminate, read and spell words with initial consonant clusters, such as 'bl', 'cr', 'tr', 'str'

title repeated from the cover

author's name listed first

non-fiction titles are usually more highly designed than fiction titles, which is why the designer's name is listed

tells you that this book is part of a series

a glossary – typical feature of a non-fiction book

at back of book

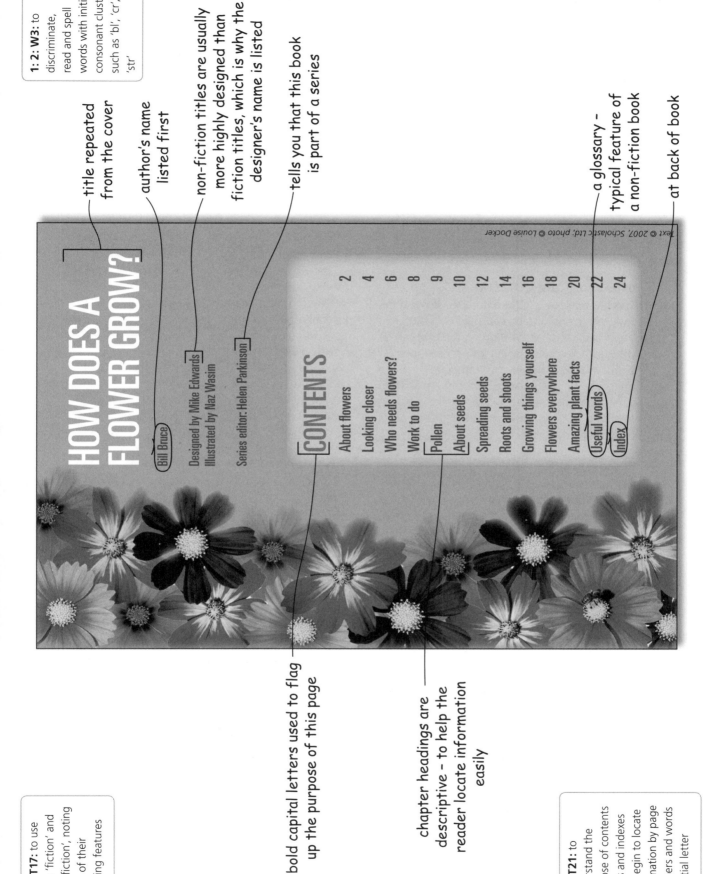

HOW DOES A FLOWER GROW?

Bill Bruce

Designed by Mike Edwards
Illustrated by Naz Wasim

Series editor: Helen Parkinson

CONTENTS

bold capital letters used to flag up the purpose of this page

chapter headings are descriptive – to help the reader locate information easily

1: 2: T17: to use terms 'fiction' and 'non-fiction', noting some of their differing features

1: 2: T21: to understand the purpose of contents pages and indexes and begin to locate information by page numbers and words by initial letter

Contents and index

by Scholastic Ltd

Background

This text encourages comparison of the purpose and organisation of contents and index pages. Differences and similarities between non-fiction and fiction texts can also be highlighted as some children begin to recognise that most information books contain an index. Take the opportunity to point out that information books do not have to be read in a linear order – a realisation that can be enticing and liberating for reluctant readers!

What's on the CD-ROM

This table can be used in a number of ways: the toy categories listed can be cut out and organised in alphabetical order; the grid can be used as a recording sheet as children interact with toys on display; the categories can be matched to pictures or photographs from catalogues; or the category words can be used to create an alternative version of the contents page in the core text.

Discussing the text

● Before sharing the text, cover the index.

● Ask the children if they know the names for different pages in a book, such as front cover, title page, acknowledgements (publishing information) and contents page. You can use a suitable non-fiction text as a model, if required.

● Show the children the contents extract and explain the meaning of the word *Contents*. Point out that the information in this book has been organised into categories – similar groups of toys – and each one is listed in the *Contents*. Demonstrate how the table format leads our eyes to the page number where we can find information about it.

● Ask the children to use the *Contents* page to answer questions such as: *What will I find out about if I look on page 6? If I want to learn about toy cars which page should I turn to? What is on page 26? If I wanted to read about Trains where should I look? What will I find on the last page listed in the contents?* The last question will lead the children to the index page which you can now reveal.

● Explain that the index gives us more specific information about how to locate individual items. Whereas the contents are listed in page order, the index items are organised in alphabetical order in a list to help the reader. Ask the children to help you check this by singing the alphabet as you highlight the letters in the index as they occur.

● Demonstrate how the information in the index can be cross-referenced to the topics in the contents page. Hide some of the page references from the index and ask the children to use the contents page to work out what the page numbers might be. Start with directly matched information, and then see whether the children can use the chapter headings to make logical guesses about sub-categories of information.

Talk, read and write

● During guided group work ask the children to locate specific words or page numbers by using the contents and index pages. Encourage more able learners to devise a question in the same style to challenge their group. Ask less able learners to focus on initial phonemes to find words beginning with, for example, 'b', 't', 'p', 'cl', 'tr', 'sk', 'pl'. Draw attention to plurals made by adding 's'.

● Involve the whole class in making a 'toy dictionary' by listing toys beginning with each letter of the alphabet accompanied by a short explanation and a drawing or photograph.

● Use the 'Toys' table provided on the differentiated text on the CD-ROM to collect information about some of the types of toys listed. The children could use reference books and the internet to research this or, if possible, visit a toy museum. Invite children to bring in some of their toys (with permission) and display these next to labels based on the categories in the grid.

● Use the toy display and the index page as a starting point to talk about how certain toys work and what they are made from.

Extension

If possible, involve parents and carers in collecting unwanted toys that can be donated to charitable organisations.

1: 2: W1: to secure identification, spelling and reading of initial, final and medial letter sounds in simple words

1: 2: W8: to investigate and learn spelling of words with 's' for plurals

note how the glossary cross-references the contents page, but additional information may also be included elsewhere in the book

note all the references to plastic toys in the book

items are listed in alphabetical order

topics are divided into sub-categories

index is set out in two columns, unlike the contents page

Index

Cars	26-7
construction kits	16-17
dolls	4-5, 14
houses	8-9
prams	18-19
felt	4
metal	13, 17, 19, 28
papier-mâché	4
plastic	5, 9, 11, 13, 15, 17, 19, 29
rubber	28
pull-along toys	20
push-along toys	20-21
tea sets	14-15
teddy bears	6-7
trains	12-13
trikes	28-9
wind-up toys	24-5

games	
board	10-11
computer	23
cup and ball	22
dice	11
drawing	23
lotto	10
skittles	10
materials	
bakelite	17
china	14, 15

CONTENTS

DOLLS	4
TEDDY BEARS	6
DOLLS' HOUSES	8
BOARD GAMES	10
TRAINS	12
TEA SETS	14
CONSTRUCTION KITS	16
PRAMS AND BUGGIES	18
TOYS ON WHEELS	20
HAND HELD GAMES	22
WIND UP TOYS	24
CARS	26
TRIKES	28
GLOSSARY	30
FURTHER READING	31
INDEX	32

indicates the page on which this subject begins

contents is organised in page order

found at the start of both fiction and non-fiction books

chapter headings used to organise and structure the information so it is easy to locate

capital letters used for each item

numbers are listed underneath each other

index appears at the end of the book

1: 2: T24: to write simple questions

1: 2: T21: to understand the purpose of contents pages and indexes and to begin to locate information by page numbers and words by initial letter

Different kinds of homes

by Melissa Mackinlay

Background

Essentially a list of different kinds of dwellings, together with pictures and some definitions, this text is a typical extract of a simple glossary that could be found at the back of an information book. The activity, which involves developing an understanding of alphabetical order and writing simple sentences, can be used alongside the following text, 'Houses and homes', page 64, which is a simple information text. Links can also be made to work on houses and homes in the history QCA Unit 2 'What were homes like a long time ago?' and to investigations of the local area in geography.

What's on the CD-ROM

The differentiated text provided on the CD-ROM has the same basic text, but contains fewer entries and is presented in non-alphabetical order. Some of the definitions have been omitted, allowing children the opportunity to create their own simple explanatory sentences.

Discussing the text

● Look at the pictures in the text and ask the children to discuss the different kinds of houses. What features distinguish them from each other? Can they name the different houses? Ask the children to make comparisons between these houses and their own homes. Do they know anyone who lives in a castle? Discuss why people live in different kinds of houses, and draw attention to some of the more unusual houses.

● Now read the text in full with the children.

● Ask the children to make observations about the layout of the text, and discuss the usefulness of including pictures as well as written text when giving information like this. Compare the information given in each entry, and encourage the children to discuss why this information has been included (to explain and 'define' each type of home). Now discuss the wider purpose of the text as a glossary. If possible, show the children examples of other glossaries from non-fiction books, and demonstrate how the glossary words are linked to key words in the book.

● Draw attention to the alphabetical ordering of the information, and, if children are familiar with other types of alphabetical texts, particularly dictionaries, ask them to make comparisons with these. A glossary can be considered a kind of mini, topic-specific dictionary.

● Take the opportunity to revise the alphabet with the children. Show the letters as you say the alphabet together. Then challenge the children with some questions about the alphabet, such as: *Which is the first letter? Which is the second letter/last letter/fifth letter and so on?*

Talk, read and write

● Using the differentiated text on the CD-ROM, focus on reorganising the words alphabetically.

● Model how to add new entries to the glossary, ensuring that you keep within the topic of 'homes' (some children might be able to suggest, for example, *apartment* or *maisonette*). Encourage the children to help you to add these in alphabetical order.

● When the list is arranged, discuss some of the words that are missing definitions. After discussion, help the children to construct sentences for the missing entries. Use the core text as a model, and talk about the importance of capital letters and full stops. Stop the children regularly to share their sentences and to talk about common errors and misconceptions as well as examples of good work.

● Reinforce children's understanding of alphabetical order by using their first names on cards or on the board and asking them to arrange groups of two, three and then four children in alphabetical order. Once a list has been arranged, introduce another child's name and ask the children to tell you where to place it in the list.

Extension

Ask children to paint pictures or take photographs of their homes for display. Support them in writing a simple caption about their home that describes what type of home it is. Encourage more able learners to include who they share their home with and why they like living there. Use the display to extend the glossary of houses and homes, ensuring that new entries are added in alphabetical order.

1: 2: T25: to assemble information from own experience

1: 2: S5: to continue demarcating sentences in writing, ending a sentence with a full stop

the first two letters are the same, so the words are ordered by the 3rd letter

words are organised in a simple list, often found at the end of an information book

key feature of text is alphabetical listing of words

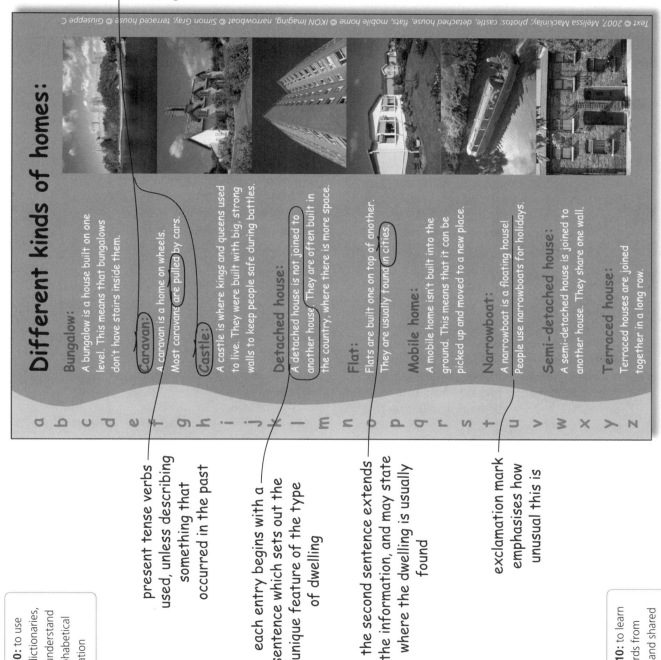

Text © 2007, Melissa Mackinlay; photos: castle, detached house, flats, mobile home © IKON Imaging, narrowboat © Simon Gray, terraced house © Giuseppe C

Different kinds of homes:

Bungalow:
A bungalow is a house built on one level. This means that bungalows don't have stairs inside them.

Caravan:
A caravan is a home on wheels. Most caravans are pulled by cars.

Castle:
A castle is where kings and queens used to live. They were built with big, strong walls to keep people safe during battles.

Detached house:
A detached house is not joined to another house. They are often built in the country, where there is more space.

Flat:
Flats are built one on top of another. They are usually found in cities.

Mobile home:
A mobile home isn't built into the ground. This means that it can be picked up and moved to a new place.

Narrowboat:
A narrowboat is a floating house! People use narrowboats for holidays.

Semi-detached house:
A semi-detached house is joined to another house. They share one wall.

Terraced house:
Terraced houses are joined together in a long row.

a
b
c
d
e
f
g
h
i
j
k
l
m
n
o
p
q
r
s
t
u
v
w
x
y
z

present tense verbs used, unless describing something that occurred in the past

each entry begins with a sentence which sets out the unique feature of the type of dwelling

the second sentence extends the information, and may state where the dwelling is usually found

exclamation mark emphasises how unusual this is

1: 2: T20: to use simple dictionaries, and to understand their alphabetical organisation

1: 2: W10: to learn new words from reading and shared experiences

Houses and homes

by Melissa Mackinlay

Background

This is another simple information text about homes and should be linked to the previous text, 'Different kinds of homes', page 62, in which children looked at an alphabetically ordered glossary about houses. This text could also be linked to work on houses and homes in history and geography. If possible, provide other texts about houses which can be used for reference during the lesson and as part of a display which children can refer to at any time for further information and for help with spellings.

What's on the CD-ROM

The differentiated text on the CD-ROM has pictures of two unusual homes with some simple questions which encourage the reader to look closely at the pictures and draw on their own preferences and experiences. These questions can be used as a prompt for discussion of any houses. Labels can be added to the pictures in the style of the core text.

Discussing the text

● Look at the text as a whole and ask the children what they can tell you about the way in which it is set out. Prompt with questions such as: *How does it differ from a story? What information might be found from it? Is it necessary to read all of the text or to read it beginning at the top left and working towards the bottom right?* If you have shared 'Different kinds of homes' with the children, compare the similarities and differences in layout, content, organisation and purpose between the two texts. Explain that, for both of these, a reader can 'pick and choose' what to read, and that one paragraph does not follow on from the previous one.

● Look at the pictures and read the captions, discussing how the words are spelled.

● Read the rest of the text in conjunction with the pictures. Ask the children questions about the different kinds of homes to check understanding, for example: *What is a semi-detached house? Where do you find blocks of flats? How is a bungalow different from a detached house?* Explore the distinction between the words *house* and *home*. (*House* generally refers to a certain type of domestic building; whereas a *home* is where someone lives.)

● Talk more about the information provided and relate the details about the specific houses to the generalised introduction about different kinds of houses (for example, *big*/*small*; *new*/*old*). Discuss how subheadings (for example, *Big houses*) could be added to organise the information further. Model adding the headings.

Talk, read and write

● Show some children the differentiated text from the CD-ROM and examine the images of the homes. Read the questions, and establish what the children already know in answer to them, and what they can find out from looking closely at the images. After discussing possible answers, encourage the children to talk about what else they would like to find out about these particular homes, and demonstrate how to formulate questions. Ensure that there are reference books and/or electronic resources available for the children to carry out further research.

● Explain that you are going to use the information from this text to add to the other text that they read earlier. Ask the children to suggest headings under which the new homes could be organised (for example, *Unusual houses*; *Holiday homes*). Model how to write the first sentence for one of the pictures, and then provide a bank of key words. Guide the children in their writing of sentences and encourage them to share information about the houses.

● Finish by asking the children to discuss which house, from all they have looked at, they would most like to live in, giving preferences for their choice.

Extension

Set up the role-play area as a tent or caravan, and allow the children to talk about what items they would need to include in the area to make the experience as realistic as possible. Encourage the children to discuss where they want their 'holiday home' to be located, and what they need to take with them. How long might they be in this particular place?

1: 2: T24: to write simple questions

introduces topic by making generalised statements about houses

captions contain information that is specific to these photos

1: 2: W10: to learn new words from reading and shared experiences

question to stimulate debate/ discussion

Houses and homes

Houses come in all sorts of shapes, sizes and designs. Some are big, some are small. Some are very old and some are new. Here are some pictures of houses and homes:

These are semi-detached houses. Semi-detached houses are joined by one wall.

Terraced houses are built in a long row. These ones have two floors.

This bungalow is made out of wood. Bungalows are houses that are all on one level.

Here is a block of flats. Flats are usually built in the middle of cities, where there isn't a lot of space. If you live at the top of a block of flats, you get a very good view of the town down below you.

Everyone's house is different. What does your home look like?

Text © 2007, Melissa Macknlay; photos: semi-detached house and flats © IKON Imaging, terraced house © Giuseppe C, bungalow © Lonnie Bradley

describe different kinds of houses

addresses the reader directly; uses friendly, conversational tone

contains a simple summing up statement

1: 2: T17: to use terms 'fiction' and 'non-fiction', noting some of their differing features

1: 2: T25: to assemble information from own experience

Squirrels

by Claire Head

Background

This is quite a challenging non-chronological report about squirrels, and consequently should be the starting point for several lessons which help children to learn how to search a non-fiction text. Activities connected to this extract could be linked to a seasonal theme or to a project on woodland animals. It can also be used in conjunction with the texts 'KWL grid: owls', page 100, and 'Owls', page 102.

What's on the CD-ROM

This more straightforward version offers more support for less able learners as it focuses simply on where squirrels live and what squirrels eat. Additional challenges are presented in a chart which classifies the squirrels' food according to the season it is available in.

Discussing the text

● Begin by asking the children to tell you what they already know about squirrels. (You could complete the first two columns of a KWL grid – *What do I know* and *What do I want to find out?* An example of a KWL grid can be found on page 102.)

● Show the children some photographs of real squirrels and explain that there are both grey squirrels (introduced to the UK from North America) and red squirrels (native to the UK) in this country. The following website is a useful source of grey squirrel pictures and video clips: www.kafox.freeserve.co.uk/fluffy/fluffy.htm.

● Read the text, pausing as necessary to talk about the technical, unfamiliar vocabulary such as *white underside, clawed feet, hibernate*. Where possible, encourage the children to draw on their own experience to explain this. Prompt with, for example: *Has anyone seen a squirrel in the park?* Use the glossary provided in the text to define specific words listed.

● Discuss what *in the shape of a football* means and hold up a real football so that the children can visualise the shape and approximate size of a *drey*.

● After reading, ask the children some questions that focus on key points made in the text. Present the questions on long strips of paper which can be attached to the board, and highlight the question words. For example, ask: *What is a drey? How big is the grey squirrel's nest? When are baby squirrels born?*

● Ask the children to discuss the questions in pairs. Take feedback from the class and then highlight where the answers can be found in the text. Show the children how important it is to scan the text for key words, such as *nest* and *drey*, when looking for specific information.

● Highlight and talk about the word *fork* (a homograph), in the third paragraph. Explain that it is a word that can have more than one meaning, but the spelling stays the same. Ask the children how it is used in the text and to suggest a different meaning.

Talk, read and write

● Chop up the text and divide it into the following sections for group work: appearance, movement, habitat, feeding. Allocate one section and one question to each group, for example: *What do squirrels like to eat? What helps the squirrel to grip slippery tree branches?* Provide support as each group discusses their answer. The earlier class work with question strips will have provided a model for this. Ask the children to present their answers as a group poster. Each group should feed back to the rest of the class in the plenary. More able leaners can take one of the section headings and think of their own question for their group.

● During shared or guided reading using an interactive whiteboard or grouped around a computer, show the children how the internet can be used to research information about squirrels. Display some key words the children could use in search engines and/or suggest suitable websites. The following is good one for children: www.wildlifetrust.org.uk/ urbanwt/education/wildlifeeducationwebsite/ squirrelsgrey.htm.

● After the initial input, opportunities to look at photographs, and time to refer to more information books, ask the children to label their own squirrel picture. Some children could create captions using simple sentences.

Extension

If possible, ask families to accompany children to a local park to spot squirrels. If the school has a bird table you could add a squirrel feeder to attract squirrels and keep them away from the birds' food!

1: 2: T22: to write labels for drawing and diagrams

report is written in present tense

each paragraph focuses on a different aspect: what they look like; how they move; where they live; what they eat; young

feature of non-fiction texts

1: 2: T25: to assemble information from own experience

introductory paragraph tells you what squirrels look like and what kind of animal they are

1: 2: T17: to use terms 'fiction' and 'non-fiction', noting some of their differing features

Squirrels

The grey squirrel has a grey back, a white underside and a bushy grey tail. They can grow up to 26cm in length. Squirrels are rodents.

Grey squirrels can leap from tree to tree. They cling on to smooth branches with their sharp clawed feet and keep their balance with their long tails. Squirrels can go down tree trunks head first. They are also able to swim.

Squirrels live in dreys. These are nests made of twigs, leaves, grass and moss rolled together in the shape of a football. Squirrels build their nests in holes inside tree trunks or in the fork of a tree.

Squirrels get most of their food from trees. They eat seeds, fruit and nuts. Sometimes they eat insects, flowers, birds' eggs and tree shoots. Squirrels do not hibernate but in winter, they dig up nuts that they have stored underground.

Baby squirrels are born in spring or in summer. The mother cares for her young who are born blind and deaf.

Glossary

Hibernate: some animals sleep through the winter months when there is not as much food available.

Rodents: a type of mammal e.g. rats, mice, voles.

Text © 2007, Claire Head; photo © Stephen Rainer

provides generalised information about all grey squirrels, not a specific individual; typical of report writing

list of items

technical vocabulary

1: 2: T24: to write simple questions

Kittens

by David Waugh

Background

This is a short information text about kittens' early lives, given in chronological order. Although it is not a recount (present and future tense verbs are used), it contains connecting words to give the writing coherence and allow it to flow in a logical way. Additional information is provided through captioned photographs. This resource can be linked to science work on humans and other animals and to work in citizenship. It can also provide a starting point for children to make more use of non-fiction texts to find out more about animals. It can be linked to 'Looking after animals', page 74 and 'The day I brought my first pet home', page 86.

What's on the CD-ROM

This differentiated text has a picture of a kitten and a wordbank of body parts. Children can use the words to label the picture, and then, after oral rehearsal, could write captions or a simple paragraph describing what the kitten looks like.

Discussing the text

● Begin by asking the children about their pets and any pets the class or school has. Does anyone have a cat? Does anyone have kittens? Can they remember what the kittens were like when they were very young? Having established what children have already experienced, explain that you are going to show them some pictures of kittens and then read an information text.

● Look at the photographs and ask the children to help you to label the *ears* and *eyes* on one of the kittens. Point to some other parts of the kittens' bodies and ask the children which words they would use to label them, for example *nose*, *whiskers* and *mouth*.

● Now read the text to and then with the children and talk about the information given. To confirm understanding, ask questions about the text such as: *Can kittens see when they are born? Can kittens hear when they are first born? What do kittens feed on when they are very young?*

● Write some of the answers that the children give in sentences on the board. Highlight the use of capital letters to begin sentences and full stops to end them. Read the sentences with the children, and ask if they would like to modify them in any way to make them sound better, or simpler. Talk about different ways of phrasing sentences.

● Look at the words *sleep* and *play*. Say them aloud with the children, breaking them into segments such as *sl-ee-p* and *pl-ay*. Highlight the initial consonant clusters and ask the children if they can think of other words which have the same beginnings. Make a list of these on the board, for example *slip, slap, slope, slam* and *please, plan, plane, plum*. During independent work, pairs of children could look for further examples, using, where appropriate, simple dictionaries or other non-fiction texts.

Talk, read and write

● Look at the differentiated text with children and read the words in the wordbank which are to become labels for parts of the kittens' body. Sound the words in segments and ask the children to repeat them. Look at the word *whiskers* and talk about other common words which begin with 'wh', such as *when, where, why, what* and *who*. Point out that these words are often found at the beginning of question sentences.

● Go on to ask the children to work in pairs to think of simple sentences about kittens. These could be sentences that describe the kittens pictured here, or they could extend the core text by going on to explain the behaviour of slightly older kittens.

● Ask the children to try writing some further sentences about cats and kittens, and guide them as they write. Remind the children about using capitals to begin sentences and full stops to end them. Stop the children regularly to share ideas, discuss spellings and to model writing sentences on the board.

Extension

Encourage children to find out more about cats and kittens and other domestic pets. They could go on to find pictures of dogs and puppies and label these. Make a display of pictures of domestic pets, encouraging children to bring in photographs and drawings of their own pets, with sentences providing information about them, such as *My dog is called Rover; We have two cats called Sifa and Poppy.*

information is provided in chronological order, beginning with information about very young cats

Text © 2007, David Waugh; photos: top © Mehmet Sensoy, centre © Armin Hanisch, bottom © Sanja Gjenero

KITTENS

Baby cats are called kittens. For the first few weeks of their lives, kittens sleep most of the time – just like human babies. Although they have eyes and ears when they are born, they cannot hear or see. They drink their mother's milk, and she keeps them safe and warm.

These kittens are three weeks old. Although they can see and hear, they stay very close to the mother cat.

When they are about 10 days old, kittens open their eyes for the first time. By the time they are three weeks old, they will start moving around. Kittens love to play!

When they are five weeks old, they start eating food. Soon they no longer need to drink milk from their mothers. It is time for the kittens to go to their new home.

At 8 weeks, this young kitten is ready to leave its mother.

introductory sentence which defines the word 'kittens'

consonant clusters

illustrates the text and makes it more visually appealing. Provides a focal point for discussion

connectives which link the recount together

The playground

by David Waugh

Background

The purpose of this text is to look at how texts can use pictures and captions to provide information. The text has labels and a few captions to demonstrate the kind of information that could be added to the pictures. Spaces are provided for children to add additional labels and captions. This text provides scope for vocabulary development in the familiar context of a park/playground, and for sentence writing, as well as for phonic work. It can be linked to an activity on playground rules and games and to the design and technology unit on playgrounds.

What's on the CD-ROM

The differentiated text provided on the CD-ROM contains the pictures from the core text and additional images, but places them as individual cut-outs. Working in pairs or groups, children can use the pictures to design their own playground, justifying the layout to each other. The purpose of the text is, in addition to encouraging creativity, to scaffold speaking and listening, using dialogue and discussion to negotiate a mutually agreed design. More able learners could add a caption explaining the design.

Discussing the text

● Talk about parks and playgrounds and ask about the children's favourite pieces of apparatus. Look at the picture of the park with the children and ask them what they can see. Ask questions such as: *How many swings are there? How many children can you see? Which piece of apparatus is nearest to the lake? Which piece of apparatus is next to the swings?* Suggest that this text could be used to tell people about the different items of equipment in a playground and how they are used.

● Look at the names of the items in the labels and read them with the children. Draw attention to the sounds which make up the words and focus, in particular, on initial consonant clusters, such as 'sl', 'tr', 'cl' and 'sw', and the final consonant digraph 'ng'. Elicit other words which have similar beginnings and list the children's suggestions in columns. Then make a list of words ending with 'ng', such as *ring, bring, thing, hang, rang, sung,* and *song.*

● Look at the text box with sentences about the seesaw and read it to and then with the children. Discuss the information provided and talk with them about their experiences of seesaws. Ask if they would like to add any further information, and if anyone would, add this to the text, discussing features of the sentence as you do so.

● Now ask the children to look at another piece of apparatus and to suggest what might be written in the caption box. Encourage them to discuss this in pairs before they share their ideas with the class. Use one of the children's suggestions to demonstrate writing a sentence, emphasising the use of capital letters and full stops. Ask the children to suggest ways of improving it by changing words, changing word order, or by adding to it.

● Repeat the exercise with either the lake or the trees, thinking aloud as you make choices about what kind of information could be included in each caption.

Talk, read and write

● Ask the children to imagine that they have never visited a playground before. What sorts of questions would they want to ask about it? Model some ideas and discuss different ways of beginning questions. Then ask the children to work in pairs to make up their own questions related to the playground. Encourage them to try out their questions on you and each other before writing some down and exchanging them for their partners to write replies.

● Show the children the differentiated text and explain how they will be able to use it. Remind the children of the rules of collaborative working, and the need to respect other people's opinions, before allowing them to begin designing their own playground in pairs or small groups.

● Select groups to present their design to the class, explaining the rationale behind their plan. Allow other children to ask questions.

Extension

Children could invent and draw their own piece of apparatus. This could be a 'fantasy' object from a futuristic playground or funfair, or it could be based on something they have seen in a park or theme park.

Text © 2007, David Waugh; illustration © Matt Ward/Beehive Illustration

1: 2: T24: to write simple questions

1: 2: W3: to discriminate, read and spell words with initial consonant clusters, such as 'bl', 'cr', 'tr', 'str'

1: 2: T23: to produce extended captions

1: 2: S6: to use the term *sentence* appropriately to identify sentences in text

playgrounds often have signs to tell you how to behave when using them

the layout of the playground is important. Equipment needs to be spaced out so it can be used safely. There may be a special area for younger children

THE PLAYGROUND

NO SWIMMING

Slide
This is a slide. You climb up the ladder to get to the top. You have to wait until no-one is in the way before you slide down.

Seesaw
There are three children playing on the seesaw. The big boy is very heavy. This is why there are two smaller boys on the other side.

slide   seesaw   lake   roundabout   trees   climbing frame   bouncy horse   swings

sub-heading provided in bold – emphasizes the name of the equipment

the purpose of the caption is to explain how the equipment works

Playground fun

from the Playground Fun website

Background

This text explains how to play the traditional singing game *Drop Handkerchief.* Evidence suggests that the game has been played in many different countries and is known by different names. It is very similar to a traditional circle game based on the nursery rhyme 'Lucy Locket'. It links to the previous text and provides many opportunities to talk about personal and social aspects of school life.

What's on the CD-ROM

A version of the traditional rhyme 'Lucy Locket' is accompanied by some questions to prompt discussion. Children can use the core text as a model to write their own instructions for this version of the game. To help children to learn this rhyme you might like to play a musical version to them. Visit www.smart-central.com/locket.htm. (The Lucy Locket tune was adopted in the American Civil War and became 'Yankee Doodle'.)

Discussing the text

● Before reading the text, ask the children to tell their talking partner what their favourite playground game is and why. Invite pairs to feed back, and scribe some the names of the games on the board. The children will hopefully realise that some of the games are very similar but are known by more than one name. Explain that sometimes the names and rules for games change over time as they are played by and taught to different people in different places.

● Present the text and tell the children that this playground game is based on a rhyme and that different versions of it have been played all over the world for centuries. Ask the children if they recognise the names and can suggest how to play the game.

● Before reading the text, highlight the name of the game and the subheadings so that the children understand that this information has been organised into different sections. If appropriate, relate these to other instructional texts the children have read.

● Now read the text in full, and discuss how it is quite difficult to remember and follow instructions until you have tried them out. Next, read and number each instruction and choose a group of children to demonstrate each stage.

The rest of the class can join in with the singing and check that the instructions have been followed.

● Check children's understanding of the word *IT,* and discuss the function of the bold type in highlighting the rhyme.

Talk, read and write

● During guided group work ask the children to recall and explain the game orally to each other and then to play it. Encourage children to remember their instructions so they can teach friends from different classes how to play this game at playtime.

● In shared or guided writing, model how to write questions about how the game is played (some might well have come up during the group work above), for example: *How many people can play? Do you need any special equipment to play?* Write the questions on large cards. Then use these to interview the children. Go on to create a display of the question cards accompanied by answers you support the children in writing.

● Ask the children to draw a picture of the game in action and to label it to explain how it is played. Provide support by taking digital photographs of the game being played and using these to sequence instructions.

● Use the differentiated text from the CD-ROM to practise instructional talking and writing. Begin by explaining how women used to keep their precious belongings in pockets which were not sewn into their clothes but were more like purses tied around the waist with ribbons or string. Thieves used to steal pockets by cutting the ribbons. Ask the children first to explain to a friend, and then write down how the game is played. (It follows the same rules as *Drop Handkerchief.*)

Extension

Ask children to research playground games. Visit the playground fun website at: www.playgroundfun.org.uk and encourage children to choose new games to learn about. Your class could submit the instructions for one of their favourite games! Children could also discover more about pockets and how they were worn by visiting www.vam.ac.uk/collections/fashion/pockets.

1: 2: **T24:** to write simple questions

photo helps reader to interpret the text

could be replaced with a personal pronoun (he/she) or a name

final instruction; indicates that the process starts again

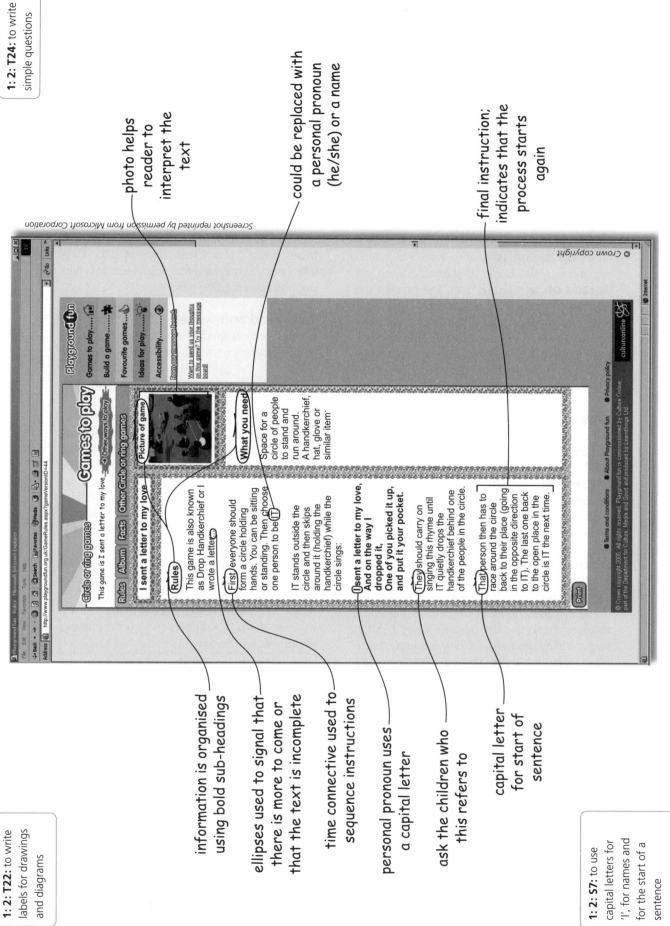

1: 2: **T22:** to write labels for drawings and diagrams

information is organised using bold sub-headings

ellipses used to signal that there is more to come or that the text is incomplete

time connective used to sequence instructions

personal pronoun uses a capital letter

ask the children who this refers to

capital letter for start of sentence

1: 2: **S7:** to use capital letters for 'I', for names and for the start of a sentence

Looking after animals

from the Connexions Direct website

Background

This text is presented as a simple set of advisory guidelines that encourage responsible pet ownership. Specific guidance given in bullet points is set within more general opening and closing paragraphs. It will provide plenty of opportunities for discussion as the children debate what each point means and why it is important. It will help the children to appreciate how much responsibility is involved in owning a pet and they will begin to learn about the job that a veterinary surgeon does. This text links to two other extracts in this book, 'Diary of a PDSA vet' on page 90 and 'Kittens' on page 68 and is a useful revision on instructional texts from Term 1. It also fits in with the citizenship QCA Unit 3 'Animals and us' and can link to science topics on animals.

What's on the CD-ROM

A writing frame in the form of a chart has been provided here. It can be used during shared, guided, or individual work time to help children to identify and present information about how to care for particular pets. The wordbank included will help children to label their drawings or to write simple sentences.

Discussing the text

● Read the title and explain to the children that this text is written for people who are thinking of getting a pet. The aim of the text is to remind people that owning a pet is a big responsibility, and should only be undertaken after they have considered this carefully. Encourage the children to talk about pets they have or care for in school. Prompt them to give examples of what they do in caring for the animals. What do the animals need to be healthy and happy?

● Read the introduction and ask the children to help you identify a letter, then a word, and then a sentence. Ask individuals to point out the capital letter at the start of the sentence and the full stop at the end.

● Read the rest of the text and help the children with the meanings of some of the more difficult specialised terminology, such as *accessories, insurance* and *reference*.

● Focus on the guidelines, and ask the children to count how many sentences are in the bulleted list. (Seven.) Point out the action words which usually occur at the start of each rule. These make the rules sound like commands and highlight how important they are.

● Ask the children to relate the text to examples from their own experience of taking a pet to the vet. Re-read the first point and discuss what is meant by the *time and energy* required to look after a pet, and what this might mean for different kinds of pets. (This will prepare children for follow-up activities using the writing frame from the CD-ROM.)

Talk, read and write

● Before re-reading, mask the high frequency words, and perhaps some of the key topic words, in the text and ask the children to identify the missing words. This could be done as a class or in guided groups.

● Involve the children in making posters to remind people about the importance of remembering the first bullet point in the text, as neglected pets soon become unwell, unhappy and potentially destructive. If you can make the necessary arrangements, perhaps these posters could be put on display in prominent sites in the local area, for example in a supermarket or library car park.

● Make a chart that tracks the care needed for a range of common pets, such as cats, dogs, rabbits, fish, stick insects. Encourage children to add to their own experience with information selected from a range of non-fiction books about animals. For example:

Pet	Home	Food	Care (owner's responsibilities)
Cat	House – a basket or cosy corner	Cat biscuits Fish Water	Playing Brushing Feeding

This chart could then be cut up and used as a matching game with questions such as *Which animal likes to eat fish?*

Extension

Talk about the work that the RSPCA does to help animals. Perhaps an RSPCA volunteer could come into school to talk to the children. You could also provide time for the children to visit the young PDSA website at http://secure.pdsa.org.uk/youngpdsa.

1: 2: T25: to assemble information from own experience

information is organised under bold sub-headings

talks to the reader directly

capital letter for start of each sentence

technical vocabulary linked to topic

bullet point for each separate piece of advice

1: 2: W10: to learn new words from reading and shared experiences

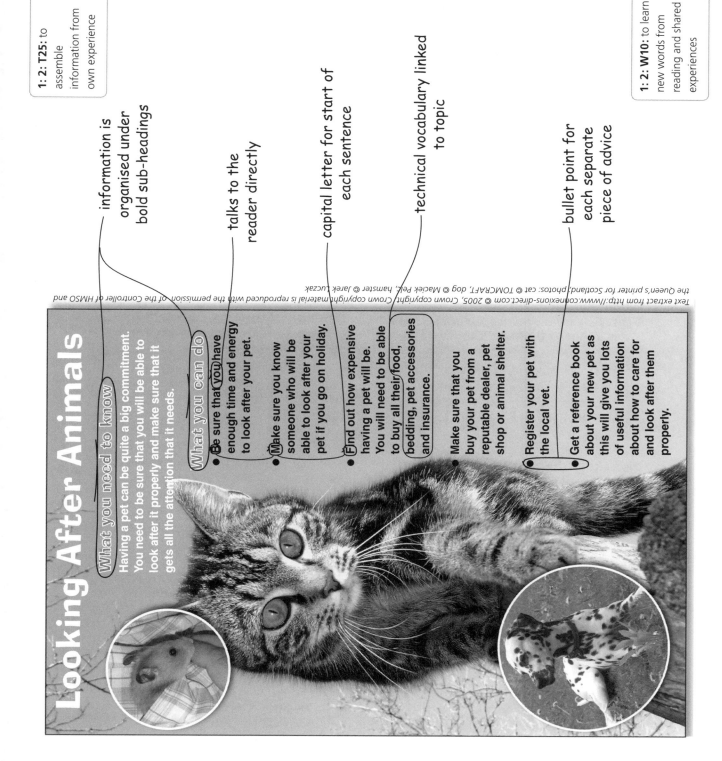

Text extract from http://www.connexions-direct.com © 2005, Crown copyright; Crown copyright material is reproduced with the permission of the Controller of HMSO and the Queen's printer for Scotland; photos: cat © TOMCRAFT, dog © Maciej Pelc, hamster © Jarek Luczak.

Looking After Animals

What you need to know

Having a pet can be quite a big commitment. You need to be sure that you will be able to look after it properly and make sure that it gets all the attention that it needs.

What you can do

- Be sure that you have enough time and energy to look after your pet.

- Make sure you know someone who will be able to look after your pet if you go on holiday.

- Find out how expensive having a pet will be. You will need to be able to buy all their food, bedding, pet accessories and insurance.

- Make sure that you buy your pet from a reputable dealer, pet shop or animal shelter.

- Register your pet with the local vet.

- Get a reference book about your new pet as this will give you lots of useful information about how to care for and look after them properly.

1: 2: T24: to write simple questions

1: 2: S6: to use the term sentence appropriate to identify sentences in text

Stay safe in the Sun

by Claire Head

Background

This information/instruction text will provide a springboard for discussion about the Sun and how Sun safety is important for health. The text can link to work in science and PSHE. You could use this text at the start of the summer term to introduce your school's Sun safety policy to the children and to alert children and parents to the importance of avoiding sunburn. For more information, visit the NGfL site: www.mindbody soul.gov.uk/safety/sun.html.

What's on the CD-ROM

A poster-style version of the *Sun safety code* is available on the CD-ROM. Children could read and discuss the code in guided reading and then work independently to illustrate each rule to help their friends understand the message that the poster communicates. With support, children can write captions to accompany their illustrations.

Discussing the text

● Tell the children that this text will help them to learn some very important information about how to stay safe in the Sun and avoid getting sunburned. Before reading, ask the children if they can tell you which months of the year are usually hot and sunny in this country. Read the months specified in the text and point out the capital letter at the start of each one.

● Continue reading, up to *Protect yourself in the sun*, pausing to let children talk about their personal experiences. For example, do they like playing outside on hot sunny days? What happens to sun cream when we go swimming? Does anyone own a pair of sunglasses?

● Highlight the acronyms *UV* and *SPF*. Ask the children if they have heard them before and if they know what they mean. Write the answers on the board and explain them. Help the children to understand how the initial capital letters are used to represent words. *UV = Ultra Violet* (the harmful light rays that come from the Sun) and *SPF = Sun Protection Factor* (the level of protection the sunscreen provides). Explain to the children that people with fair skin need a higher level of SPF protection from the Sun as they are more susceptible to sunburn. To stay healthy we all need to avoid sunburn as this damages our skin.

● Before reading the *Protect yourself in the sun* section, ask the children to think, pair and share about how they can do this. After feedback shared as a class, read the list and relate each point to the school environment. For example, Where are the shady spots in the school grounds? Do the children know how to put on their own sun cream? Who remembers to wear a hat to school on sunny days?

Talk, read and write

● Use the differentiated version of the text as the starting point to help children design their own posters to be displayed around the school. Encourage the children to draw labelled diagrams which illustrate the Sun safety code.

● Take the children outside to identify what happens when the Sun goes behind a cloud. Some children may think that this is what happens when night falls. Explain to the children that the sun is still a source of light even if it is hidden for a few minutes from our view because it is behind a cloud. (Remind the children that the text warned them about the danger of looking directly at the Sun.)

● Challenge the children to identify the changes that have been made to the spelling of the action words at the start of each sentence in the Sun safety code compared to the spelling of these words in the main text ('ing' endings, for example *cover – covering*). As an additional challenge, ask the children to tell you what happens to the word *rub* or *swim* when 'ing' is added, for example *rubbing in your sun cream* or *swimming in the sea*.

● During guided group work, help the children to use the letters *SUN* as the starting point for their own Sun safety code or sun facts. For example, *Sun cream is important; Under a tree is shady; Necks need protecting.*

Extension

On sunny days, involve the children in checking the solar UV index level at the end of television forecasts or on the Met Office website: www.metoffice.gov.uk/weather/uv/index.html.

1: 3: **T21**: to use the language and features of non-fiction text

1: 3: **S5**: to know other common uses of capitalisation

fun image of sun used as bullet points

acronym, stands for 'sun protection factor'

names of months start with capital letters

reader is addressed directly

keeps tone light and friendly

acronym, stands for 'ultra-violet'

points to remember about sun safety written as an acrostic

STAY SAFE IN THE SUN

Summer sunshine

You can get sunburned if you don't take care in the following months of the year:

| April | May | June | July | August | September |

In the UK the sun is at its hottest between 11.00am and 3.00pm.

You need to take care whenever you are outdoors as you can get sunburned on sunny days and cloudy days!

It is dangerous to look directly at the sun because it is very bright and can burn your eyes.

Be extra careful when you go swimming in the sea or in an outdoor pool as the sun's UV rays reflect off the water and you can become sunburned very quickly. You must use a water-resistant sun cream.

Remember:

Shade is good
Use sunscreen
No burning!
Cover up
Own a hat
Drink water
Enjoy the sunshine!

Protect yourself in the sun by:

- Applying a high factor sunscreen (SPF 15+)
- Staying out of the sun in the middle of the day
- Covering up with long-sleeved shirts and long shorts
- Wearing a hat to keep the sun off your head and neck
- Looking out for shady spots e.g. under trees
- Drinking plenty of water to avoid getting dehydrated.

1: 3: **W6**: to investigate and learn spellings of verbs with 'ed' (past tense) and 'ing' (present tense) endings

1: 3: **W8**: to learn new words from reading and shared experiences

Make a string telephone

by Scholastic Ltd

Background

Predominantly an instructional text, this extract also includes a short explanation of the science behind the experiment. The text contains a range of presentational devices which are often found in non-fiction books: photographs; numbered instructions; subheadings. Additional work surrounding sound and hearing could be explored as part of a science topic.

What's on the CD-ROM

This template can be used to scaffold children's own instructions. Less able learners could use the headings to support spoken instructions, while more able could then go on to write their own version of the core text.

Discussing the text

● Tell the class that you are going to conduct an experiment to find out how sound travels as we cannot see it. Explain that we can hear it through our ears but before that it first travels through the air or solid objects. Sound seems louder the nearer you are to the source. Sounds are fainter the further away you are from the source. Explain that you are going to share some instructions to learn how to make a string telephone.

● Read the heading: *Make a string telephone.* Read steps 1 and 2 carefully, pausing to ensure that the children have understood each separate task. Carry out the instruction and talk about the health and safety hazards involved in piercing the cup. Ask the children to think, pair and share ideas about how this task could be done safely.

● Read steps 3 and 4 and then model how to carry out these instructions. You could make a mistake and knot both ends of the string before feeding one end through the cup. This will highlight how important it is to follow the instructions carefully.

● Read step 5. Discuss potential problems as you continue to make the example telephone. For example, felt-tipped pens might not show up on a plastic cup, so what other method could the children use to decorate the cup? Or consider using (more environmentally friendly) paper cups instead.

● Finally read the last three instructions.

● Now draw attention to the layout of the text. Discuss why there are numbers next to each paragraph. Ask whether the experiment would work if you tried to carry out the steps in another order.

● Choose a child to help you test the string telephone. Tell the children that they are going to make their own telephones and will need to find out if the information in the text is correct. Read the *How it works* section. To make this explanation more visual you could demonstrate the vibrations by hitting a drum. If you place small pieces of tissue paper on the drum the children will see these jump as the vibrations travel through the taut drum skin when you hit it.

Talk, read and write

● Ask the children to work in pairs to make their own string telephone by following the shared instructions.

● Let the children test their string telephones. Ask pairs to report back in the plenary to explain how they worked together and what they found out.

● Challenge the children to draw themselves using their string telephone to talk to a friend. Ask each child to label the diagram and to explain (by drawing, writing simple sentences or talking to an adult) how the sound travels from one person to the other.

● Chop up the instructions and remove the numbers. Ask children to work in small guided groups to re-order these and add some helpful illustrations to support each stage. This could be presented as an A3 poster. More able learners could add further instructions to their poster to help avoid some of the mistakes that you might have made! Ask the children to add a health and safety warning to their version of the instructions. Encourage them to think about a good way to present this (for example, in a red warning triangle) as it needs to stand out. These posters could be put on display or used by another class.

Extension

Challenge children to find out who invented the telephone.

1: 3: S4: to have grammatical awareness about word order

photo supports the text

provides extra information

Text © 2007, Scholastic Ltd; photos © 2006, Jupiter Images Corporation

Make a String Telephone

1. Find two disposable plastic cups.
2. Poke a very small hole in the bottom of each with a sharp pencil.
3. Feed string through the holes in each cup.
4. Tie a knot at each end of the string and pull the cups to check they don't come off.
5. Decorate both cups using coloured pens.
6. Work with a partner, and pull the cups taut.
7. Put a cup to your ear and ask your partner to talk into theirs.
8. Can you hear what your partner is saying?

How It Works

The string carries sounds as tiny vibrations, which you can feel if you touch the string. The cup allows your ear to hear these vibrations as sounds.

informative title tells you the purpose of the instructions

numbered steps organise the instructions so they are easy to follow

short, simple sentences

explanation sub-heading in yellow

1: 3: T17: to recognise that non-fiction books on similar themes can give different information and present similar information in different ways

1: 3: T21: to use the language and features of non-fiction texts

Why parks attract wildlife

by Ralph Whitlock

Background

This challenging extract is taken from a book called *Use your eyes: in the Park*. Although the text is entitled 'Why parks attract wildlife', it is a report-type text rather than an explanation. You will need to read it to the children before they look at it, being ready to discuss some of the words which may be new to them. The lesson can be linked to 'Trip to the park', page 92, and to 'House sparrows', page 82 and 'Garden birds', page 84. It ties in with the science topics 'Humans and other animals' and 'Living things in their environment'.

What's on the CD-ROM

The differentiated text uses simple statements accompanied by pictures which provide children with clues to help them to read less familiar words. Children can use the pictures as a prompt to ask questions, and to draw and write about parks, while the text can be used as a model for writing.

Discussing the text

● Explain to the children that they are going to look at an extract from a book about parks and that this extract focuses on wildlife. Before reading the text to them and then with them, talk about a park's different environments and ask about some of the wild creatures you might expect to see in the park. What might they find in the trees, ponds and lakes or in open spaces? What kinds of foods can wild creatures find in a park? Write *environment* on the board and explain that it means the surroundings in which we and other creatures and plants live. The word is phonically regular and children will enjoy learning a long word, so break the word into segments (*en-vi-ron-ment*) and help children to say it and learn how to spell it.

● Now read the first paragraph to the children and discuss and write up some of the less familiar words, such as *wildlife*, *environment*, *singly*, *grassy* and *Usually*. Then read the paragraph together.

● Do the same with the second paragraph, explaining words such as *search*, *country*, *bushes*, *creatures* and *bathing*.

● Write *What*, *Where*, *Why*, *When* and *Who* on the board, and tell the children you are going to make up questions using these words.

Read the two paragraphs again with the children and model how to make up questions related to the text. For example: *Where do birds and animals often search for food? Why do you think creatures hide? What sort of animals live in parks?* Highlight the question words at the beginning and the question marks at the end.

● Now read the final paragraph and discuss words such as *dense*, *fields*, *easily* and *tame*.

● When exploring new words, look for opportunities for the children to apply their existing phonic knowledge and vocabulary to help them to read new words, as well as using what they learn about new words to help them read other words. For example, in looking at *tame*, talk about words such as *name, fame* and *lame*; and when looking at *easily*, talk about *easy, easier* and *ease*.

Talk, read and write

● Show the children the simplified text and read it with them. Discuss each sentence and ask the children to think of questions which could be answered by reading the text. These may be similar to those discussed earlier, but use the opportunity to reinforce understanding of question sentences and the use of question marks. Organise the children to work in pairs to create questions for other pairs to answer using the text.

● Model writing sentences for these answers, and make occasional mistakes which the children should alert you to, such as missing out full stops or capital letters. Read and re-read the sentences with the children and encourage them to suggest ways in which they could be improved.

Extension

Ask children to observe wildlife at home or in the park with parents and carers and to make a chart of creatures they have seen and the places where they were spotted. Create a display with a map of the locality and cards with details of birds and animals which the children have seen in different environments.

1: 3: **T22:** to write own questions prior to reading for information and to record answers

1: 3: **S7:** to add question marks to questions

photo illustrates that human intervention (e.g. feeding animals in parks) encourages them to become used to humans

describes a typical park

explains what kind of habitat is preferred by birds and animals

contains two opposing ideas, linked by the connective 'but'

1: 3: **W6:** to investigate and learn spellings of verbs with 'ed' and 'ing' endings

1: 3: **T19:** to identify simple questions and use text to find answers

1: 3: **W8:** to learn new words from reading and shared experiences

heading in large, bold font for emphasis; heading introduces topic

photo of a typical park scene to provide a point of reference for the text

opening sentence provides a link between heading and body of text

present tense verbs are a feature of reports

word in bold because it is new vocabulary

generalised references to categories of objects, not individual or named places

summarises why you are more likely to see wildlife in parks than in the countryside

1: 3: **W1:** to know the common spelling patterns for each of the long-vowel phonemes: 'ee', 'ai', 'ie', 'oa', 'oo'

Why parks attract wildlife

A park is one of the best places to see wildlife. This is because a park offers so many different **environments**. There are many kinds of trees, some standing singly and some in groups. There are also open spaces and grassy paths. Usually there is a lake, pond or a river:

Birds and animals often search for food in open country, but when they are not feeding they hide in trees or bushes, where they can watch what is happening around them. Nearly all wild creatures need to have water for drinking and bathing.

In the countryside, there will be more wild creatures in places which are like parks than in dense woods or open fields. But in the park you will be able to see them more easily, because they become used to people and so are often quite tame.

Text extract from "Use your eyes: in the Park", by Ralph Whitlock © 1986, Wayland (Publishers) Limited); photos: park © Marthy Marag, squirrel © Mister Eels, duck © Cathy Kaplan, children © Horton grou, swan © Derek Z

House sparrows

by David Waugh

Background

This simple information text comprises a picture with two parts of a sparrow labelled, another picture to illustrate a sparrow sitting on its nest, and a short paragraph of text. This is an ideal introductory lesson to the texts 'Garden birds', page 84 and 'Owls', page 102. It can also be linked to science work on life processes and animals.

What's on the CD-ROM

The differentiated text provided on the CD-ROM comprises a picture of a bird and a wordbank of key words which can be used to label the picture. It also contains a small writing frame, with questions, to prompt discussion. Together they work as a simple speaking frame to scaffold group talk and writing about what the children have learned about sparrows.

Discussing the text

● Begin by encouraging the children to talk about their experience of seeing birds at home and/or in the wild. Where did they see them? Do they know which birds they saw? Did they see any sparrows?

● Now look at the text with the children and ask them to identify three ways in which information is provided (pictures, labels and a paragraph of text). Ask them to look at the partially labelled picture and talk with them about how other parts of the bird could be labelled. Write some words on the board with their help and check the spellings. Suggestions might include *leg, claw, beak, belly, head* and *tail.*

● Read the text to the children and then with them, and discuss the information it provides. To check their understanding, ask questions such as: *Where do sparrows build their nests? How are the eggs kept warm? How long does it take from the eggs being laid for sparrows' babies to hatch out? What do sparrows eat?*

● Discuss further information about sparrows and other birds which the children can provide. Prompt them by asking, for example: *Do you put food out for birds at home? What kinds of food do the birds eat? Do you know the names of some other common birds?* You could make a list of the ones they know the names of and ask them to find out more from books at school, websites or resources at home.

● Write up on the board some of the details that the children provide. Check spellings as you do so and draw attention to common spelling patterns. Look at the word *seeds,* for example, and ask the children to look for other words with the long vowel digraph 'ee' (*see* and *week*). Ask the children to suggest other 'ee' rhyming words, and write these down.

● Go on to talk about how many common words have the same sounds represented by different spellings. If possible, look at *claw* and at other 'aw' words with an 'or' sound (*thaw, gnaw, jaw, law* and so on) and other common words with a sound represented by different graphemes (*or, four, for, store, score…*).

Talk, read and write

● Show the labelled picture on the core text and remind the class that labels sometimes have lines or arrows joining the words to the parts of the diagram that they are labelling. Provide the children with copies of the sparrow picture from the differentiated text and ask them to use the words provided to label it.

● Ask the children to work in pairs to read and discuss the questions in the grid. More able learners could scribe simple answers to the questions. Encourage children to add their own question and answer.

● Write some example answers on the board and occasionally miss out capital letters or full stops to encourage children to spot errors.

Extension

Children may wish to be involved with Birdweb from the RSPB (www.rspb.org.uk/science/birdweb), which conducts surveys of the UK's birds. They could look at this and other sites to find out more about birds.

Ask them to look out for birds at home and to note those they see. Provide a simple chart to help to identify the most common birds. (The RSPB's 2006 survey listed the most common garden birds as: 1. house sparrow; 2. starling; 3. blackbird; 4. blue tit; 5. chaffinch; 6. greenfinch; 7. collared dove; 8. woodpigeon; 9. great tit; 10. robin.)

1: 3: T21: to use the language and features of non-fiction texts

general introductory comment; classifies sparrow as a species of bird

what they eat

where they nest

raising young

1: 3: S6: to learn through reading and writing, to reinforce knowledge of term *sentence* from previous terms

written in present tense

long vowel phoneme 'oo'

long vowel phoneme 'ee'

House Sparrows

House sparrows are among the birds we can see almost anywhere in the country. They eat seeds and food which people have put out for them. They build nests near to houses under roofs and next to drainpipes. The mother sparrow lays her eggs and then keeps them warm by sitting on them. Two weeks after the eggs are laid the baby sparrows hatch out of them.

wing

eye

labelled diagram provides additional information about appearance

Text © 2007, David Waugh; photos: background © Deborah Frans, inset © Luis Rock

1: 3: T17: to recognise that non-fiction books on similar themes can give different information and present similar information in different ways

1: 3: W1: to know the common spelling patterns for each of the long vowel phonemes: 'ee' 'ai' 'ie' 'oa' 'oo'

Garden birds

by David Waugh

Background

This non-chronological text provides information about four commonly found garden birds, with information about their behaviour linked to clear illustrations of each bird. Ideally, other information texts about common British birds should be made available, including, if possible, access to internet sites. A collection of pictures of birds will also be helpful and could be incorporated into a display of children's writing about birds. This text is ideally suited to follow on from 'House sparrows' on page 82 and to any work developed on birds in the garden. The topic ties in with science work on 'humans and other animals' and 'living things in their environment'.

What's on the CD-ROM

The differentiated text provided on the CD-ROM provides further examples of common garden birds set out in a grid along with column headings in the form of question prompts to support research. Less able learners could draw pictures and write simple captions from their research, while more able could use this grid as a writing frame to plan a simple report.

Discussing the text

● Look at the pictures of the birds with the children and ask them which ones they recognise. If appropriate, recall previous reading and discussions around the text 'House sparrows'. Discuss the appearances of the birds in some detail, including colours if known, and create a list of useful words which children use to describe them. Encourage the class to help you with spellings as you write on the board.

● Talk about the information which is provided for *Swallows* and point out that, unlike the other birds, swallows leave Britain at the end of the summer. Introduce the word *migrate* and explain what it means. Now discuss *Blue Tits* and ask the children what they can tell you about them from their own experience: Do they put out food for birds in winter? Have they seen blue tits feeding? Compare the type of information for blue tits with that for swallows and discuss how it is different. (For example, the text on blue tits doesn't tell you what a blue tit looks like, or whether it migrates.) Make notes of some information from books and the internet, as well as that which is provided in the text and, with the children's help, write some sentences about blue tits suitable for a non-chronological report.

● Read the other two descriptions aloud with the children. Then, with the whole text in view, ask some comprehension questions which will focus children's attention on the text.

● Now ask the children to make up some questions of their own to ask partners and then to share with the class. Write some of these on the board and talk about the importance of using a question mark instead of a full stop to make it clear to the reader that the sentence is a question.

● Look at some examples of the long vowel phonemes with which children are becoming familiar. Common long vowel digraphs can be found in words such as *snail, tail, beak* and *eat*; while split vowel digraphs can be found in *stone, male* and *like*. When examining these words, ask the children if they can suggest other words with similar rimes. Write these on the board, drawing attention to examples of the same sound being made by different letters, for example 'ee' and 'ea', and 'ay', 'ai' and 'a–e'.

Talk, read and write

● Use the differentiated text to model how to research and note down information for one of the birds listed in the table. Show how information can be captured by using words, sentences or labelled diagrams. Encourage more able learners to turn the information into short paragraphs about birds.

Extension

Encourage children to find out more about birds, including rarer British birds and those which are not found in Britain. Ask them to make brief notes at home or at school on what they find, and to include a colour illustration or photograph. Help them to produce a display with pictures of birds and brief descriptions. These captions can be produced as a shared writing activity.

Text © 2007, David Waugh; photos: feather © Marion Herrmann; swallow © Helga Kupcsik, blue tit © Christophe Libert, song thrush © Christina Ericsson, blackbird © Cheryl Empey

1: 3: T19: to identify simple questions and use text to find answers

1: 3: W1: to know the common spelling patterns for each of the long vowel phonemes: 'ee', 'ai', 'ie', 'oa', 'oo'

text organised under clear sub-headings

interesting information about the birds' behaviour

tells you where the bird nests

long vowel phoneme 'ie'

long vowel phoneme 'ee'

long vowel phoneme 'ai'

1: 3: W7: to spell common irregular words from Appendix List 1

GARDEN BIRDS

SWALLOWS

Swallows catch insects as they are flying. Swallows have long tails. Often we see martins too, but they have shorter tails. Swallows and martins fly to warmer countries for the winter but return in the summer.

BLUE TITS

Blue tits often make nests in gardens. They like to feed on nuts which people hang up in nets. Some people put up bird boxes for blue tits to nest in.

SONG THRUSHES

Thrushes dig for worms and also look for snails to eat. They break the snails' shells by bashing them on a stone and then eat the snail inside. They have speckled chests.

BLACKBIRDS

Blackbirds dig for worms with their beaks. The males sing so that they can attract females. They also sing to tell other male blackbirds to keep away.

1: 3: T17: to recognise that non-fiction books on similar themes can give different information and present similar information in different ways

1: 3: T22: to write own questions prior to reading for information and to record answers

each section includes information about what the bird eats

information about the bird's appearance is given here

1: 3: S7: to add question marks to questions

The day I brought my first pet home
by Claire Head

Background

This recount about a child's first pet will appeal to young children and will act as a springboard for discussion on personal experiences of pet ownership. The text provides a model for recount writing as it follows a simple structure and makes good use of subheadings to organise the information. The first part of the recount describes how a girl (Saima) goes to a pet shop with her mother and buys a rabbit. She names the rabbit *Twitcher* and returns home with her. The girl continues her recount by describing how she cares for her pet.

What's on the CD-ROM

This simpler version of the recount focuses on the sequencing of key events. The subheadings have been transformed into questions and are accompanied by pictures. You could use the questions and visual prompts to discuss caring for Twitcher with the children and to write labels and captions next to the pictures.

Discussing the text

● Before reading the text, ask the children to put their hands up if they have a pet and tell you what kind of animal it is. (Someone might own a rabbit and consequently will be the expert!) Discuss the differences between animals that are kept as pets and animals that live in the wild (rabbits can, of course, be both).

● Next ask the children to think, pair and share what they know about rabbits. It may be helpful to show the children a picture and briefly describe what sort of animal it is.

● Tell the children that they are going to read a recount which describes a girl called Saima and her pet rabbit. Explain that the purpose of a recount is to retell a series of events and in this text Saima has just bought her rabbit and is telling us how she feeds, cleans and cares for her pet.

● Read the text, pausing to point out the subheadings and the way that the pictures and the text give us information.

● After sharing the full text, ask the children some questions about the information in the recount, for example: *What does Twitcher like to eat?* Then ask: *How did you find the answer?* Talk about how a reader can read and remember information in words or can use the pictures. Explain that the subheadings can also give us clues and help us to locate the part of the text we need in order to answer a specific question. Practise this technique by asking the children to listen to your next question and tell their partner which subheading will point them in the right direction. Ask, for example, *What do rabbits like to have in the bottom of their hutch to help keep it clean?* (The children should pick out the key word *hutch* from the subheadings.)

Talk, read and write

● Share thoughts about and agree on another pet that the class would like to find out about. Organise small groups and ask them to think of questions to ask about this animal. After some oral rehearsal the children could write one question each, or you could act as a scribe for the group. Remind the children to use a question mark. If a child in the class owns this type of pet, the children could take it in turns to ask the owner their questions.

● Play a game which involves using cut-up sentences from the recount. Provide questions and ask the children to work in pairs to read the questions and find the answer.

● Ask the children to write their own recounts about caring for an animal. You could model this during shared writing and then provide writing frames for the children to complete during guided writing. Organise the children to work in pairs to ensure everyone in the class has someone to talk to who has experience of caring for a pet. Encourage the children to use time connectives to help sequence their recounts, and list some on the board, for example *First, Then, Next, Finally.* This could be the starting point for a class book about 'Our pets'.

Extension

Ask children to talk to family and friends about pets they have cared for.

50 Shared texts Non-fiction ● **Year 1**

1: 3: T19: to identify simple questions and to use text to find answers

1: 3: W2: to read on sight high frequency words

1: 3: S7: to add question marks to questions

concluding statement; indicates feelings (personal reflection)

uses a variety of sentence beginnings to maintain interest

includes characters who were significant

written in 1st person

informative heading: use of personal pronoun 'I' tells reader this is a recount

follows recount procedure and establishes 'who', 'when', 'where', 'what', 'why'

sub-headings structure the writing making it easy to locate information

use of time connectives to help sequence events. Events are retold in sequence

uses action verbs

1: 3: T18: to read recounts and begin to recognise generic structure

1: 3: T21: to use the language and features of non-fiction texts

The Day I Brought My First Pet Home

Going to the pet shop yesterday morning my mum and I went to the pet shop to buy my first pet. I was very excited. I have always promised that I pet – I know there will be lots of work to do!

Choosing a pet

It was very difficult to choose a pet but eventually I picked a small, white rabbit. He was hopping around and twitching his nose when I saw him. I decided to call him Twitcher!

Buying special equipment

The pet shop owner explained that I would need some special equipment in order to care for my rabbit. I bought a hutch, some sawdust, some straw, a dish and a water bottle.

Preparing the hutch

When I got home my mum helped me to prepare the hutch. First we lined the bottom of the hutch with old newspaper. Then I poured some sawdust on top. Next I spread some hay across the bottom of the hutch to make sure Twitcher stayed warm and comfortable. I will need to clean the hutch out every week and make sure my rabbit has some clean straw.

Food and drink

My mum filled up the water bottle for me and then I fixed it in place inside the hutch. Next I cut up some carrots, celery and apples and put them on a plastic dish in the hutch. I like carrots too so I saved one for a snack. I will need to feed Twitcher every day before I go to school.

Twitcher is home

Finally it was time to show Twitcher his new home. I carefully placed him in the hutch and closed the door. Twitcher hopped around and then ate a piece of celery. Then he twitched his nose at me through the hutch door. I think he liked his new home.

Text © 2007, Claire Head; photos © 2006, Jupiter Images Corporation

Who cooks my school dinner?

by Claire Head

Background

This longer text recounts events that usually occur in the everyday life of a school cook. The scene is set by *Mrs Patrick* (the cook) who introduces herself to the reader and prepares him or her for the information, in the form of her daily schedule, which follows. The information is explained by Mrs Patrick, in the first person, in chronological order. Visual information is provided by the clock faces which display the time each new event takes place. This text can be used in conjunction with 'School dinner menu', page 34 and 'Recipe: fruit salad' on page 36.

What's on the CD-ROM

The core text has been reduced here to simple, key sentences which explain what the school cook does each day. You could use this differentiated version to help children to sequence events and to insert more information by drawing pictures to match each part of the cook's working day.

Discussing the text

● Read the title and point out the question mark. Ask the children which of them stays for school dinner, who has a packed lunch and who goes home for their lunch. Talk about the words *lunch* and *dinner* which can both be used to describe the meal most people eat around midday.

● Introduce the text and tell the children that it explains what the school cook does every day in order to prepare school dinners. Draw children's attention to the layout of the text and its different features. Explain that the information about each part of the cook's day is presented in two different ways: text and 'time pictures'.

● Read the text through, pausing to talk about what each section means and to identify personal pronouns (*I, we*) and capital letters (for names, places, start of sentences).

● Re-read the text, omitting the introduction, and ask the children to help you to title each section by thinking of subheadings that summarise the different events. For example: paragraph 1 – *Getting ready*; 2 – *Preparation*; 3 – *Cooking and setting tables*; 4 – *Serving*; 5 – *Cleaning up*. Write these on the text.

● Next, tell the children that a good recount should help the reader to answer questions, beginning with the following words: *Who? What? When? Where? How? Why?* List these question words on the board and tell the children that they are going to use the text and the subheadings to help find answers to your questions. Use the listed question words to start questions such as: *Who is the school cook? What is the first thing she does when she arrives at school? When is lunch served? How many children have a school dinner at Mrs Patrick's school?* Model the process of reading the first question then scanning the subheadings. Then allow the children to think, pair and share in order to answer the other questions.

Talk, read and write

● Use the differentiated version of the text to make a sequencing game to be played during guided reading. Cut the text into sections and read each section, in random order, with the children. Encourage them to work together to re-read each part and to think logically to discuss and decide on the correct sequence.

● Invite your school cook to come and talk to the children about his or her work. Prepare questions with the children beforehand: help pairs during guided group work to devise and write a question to ask the visitor. Remind the children about the use of a question word with a capital letter to start the question and a question mark at the end of it. Following the visit, the children could write a thank-you note for the school cook and his/her team.

● Prepare a simple dish with a group or the class (fruit salad, for example). Then, after some oral rehearsal, ask the children to write their own recount of this experience. Use the subheadings devised earlier to create a writing frame to help children structure their recounts. Perhaps also provide sentence prompts by writing temporal connectives under each subheading (*First, Then, Next, Finally*). Remind the children to explain *who, what, where, when* and *how*.

Extension

Ask children to interview someone at home about his or her day.

Text © 2007, Claire Head; photos: notepad © Davide Guglielmo, clock © Sanja Gjenero, cook © 2006, Jupiter Images Corporation

WHO COOKS MY SCHOOL DINNER?

My name is Mrs Patrick and I am the cook at Fairhaven Primary School. With the help of a team of people, I cook lunch for one hundred children every school day. There is a lot to do! Here is my busy schedule:

First, I wash my hands and put on my apron and hat. Next I make a cup of tea. I talk with my team about the menu for the day. We make a list of the food we need.

Then we prepare the food. We follow the recipe carefully to make sure we have enough food for everyone. We try to choose healthy meals.

Now we turn the huge ovens on and start cooking. When lunch is almost ready we set the tables in the school dinner hall. We put a water jug and some cups on each table.

At midday we begin serving lunch to the children. They collect their own plates and cutlery. Everyone is hungry and some people want a second helping.

After lunch we clear up. It takes a long time to wash up and clean the kitchen ready for the next day. When we have finished I am usually ready for another cup of tea!

1: 3: T19: to identify simple questions and use text to find answers

first paragraph tells you who, what, where, when. Ask questions, e.g. Who is the school cook? What is the first thing she does when she arrives at school? When is lunch served? How many children have a school dinner at Mrs. Patrick's school?

colon introduces the daily schedule

1: 3: S5: to know other common uses of capitalisation, such as for personal titles, headings, book titles, emphasis

exclamation to finish off recount

1: 3: T18: to read recounts and begin to recognise generic structure

first paragraph slightly larger to differentiate it from the actual recount

capital letters for proper nouns (names)

conversational tone; sounds as if Mrs Patrick is speaking directly to the reader

uses first person pronouns: this is a first person recount

time connectives used to order the events and make sure the writing flows

1: 3: T20: to write simple recounts linked to topics of interest/study or to personal experience

Diary of a PDSA vet

by Steve Howard

Background

This personal recount describes an eventful morning in the life of vet Steve Howard. It is presented in the form of a diary entry available on the PDSA website. Typical features of recounts include: explanation of the setting, background information, description of events in chronological order, and a concluding statement which communicates the author's feelings. This text shows how recount writing can offer us an interesting glimpse into another person's life. Children will enjoy reading this mini real-life adventure about Duggie the dog. Other texts on this topic include 'The day I brought my first pet home', page 86 and 'Looking after animals', page 74.

What's on the CD-ROM

The writing frame provided here can be used during shared, guided or independent writing to scaffold children's rewriting of this recount or writing of their own recounts. Children can also use the sentences to help in sequencing events when retelling the recount.

Discussing the text

● Explain to the children that this extract is from a vet's diary and it describes what happened to him one morning on his way to work. Ask the children if they can tell you what a vet does.

● Ask the children if they can scan the text and find the name of the vet. Read the byline giving the vet's name, his job title and where he works. Explain the acronym *PDSA* (People's Dispensary for Sick Animals) and talk about *vet* being a shortened form of *veterinary surgeon*.

● Read the recount to the children, pausing to ask them to predict what they think happened next at crucial stages. Point out the use of the first person pronouns *I* and *we*, which tells us that it is the vet himself who is explaining what happened. Highlight the words and phrases that convey the sense of urgency the vet felt as he tried to help the dog and get him to hospital quickly.

● Ask children to point out some of the capital letters in the extract, and discuss the different purposes: to indicate the start of a sentence, and to flag up a name, job role or organisation.

● After reading, draw attention to the way this short text has provided detailed information about the vet and his morning, for example how he gets to work, where he encountered the dog in distress, the journey to the hospital, how he treated the dog.

● Next, re-read the text slowly and this time ask the children to sketch the events as they unfold (on individual whiteboards or storyboard grids). When you have finished reading ask the children to number their drawings in the order the events occurred and then use this to help to retell the vet's busy morning to a partner. Encourage the children to use time connectives *first, then, next, after that, finally.*

Talk, read and write

● Make flashcards with the question words *who, what, where, how* and *why.* Fix these to the board and ask the children to help you to answer them by re-reading the text. Once the children are familiar with this and recognise how to listen for and locate specific information, give out the flashcards to groups and ask them (with support) to find the answers and report back to the class.

● Ask the children to retell an event concerning their own pets or other animals they have come into contact with. Encourage the children to include talk about how important it is to care for animals properly.

● Use the differentiated text from the CD-ROM to make sentence cards for the children to re-order. Then ask the children to work in pairs to write their own sequence of events using the recount writing frame.

● During guided group work, access the Young PDSA website (http://secure.pdsa.org.uk/youngpdsa) and read further recounts about individual pets and how they have been helped at the PetAid hospital. You could send off for an education pack from the site.

Extension

If possible, visit a local veterinary hospital or invite a vet to the school to talk to the children about his or her days at work.

1: 3: T19: to identify simple questions and use text to find answers

capital letter to indicate name of hospital

explains who/what/where/how and implies why

connective to link events; sets the scene for the next event

all suggest urgency of situation

technical vocabulary linked to topic

exclamation to conclude recount on a humorous note – and reassure the reader that all is well

1: 3: S5: to know other common uses of capitalisation, such as for personal titles, headings, book titles, emphasis

Screenshot reprinted by permission from Microsoft Corporation

PDSA I for pets in need of vets - Microsoft Internet Explorer

File Edit View Favorites Tools Help

Back ▾ Search Favorites

Address http://secure.pdsa.org.uk/youngpdsa/reggie_4.php Go Links

Diary of a PDSA vet

Morning

I set off a bit early today, as I've got quite a bit to do at the PetAid hospital. I've also bought myself a new bicycle, which I'm dying to try out! Dressed in all of the safety gear I start off towards the hospital.

As I cycle through the park I see a lady who is very upset. She's been out with her dog, throwing sticks and one has got stuck in her dog's throat. The dog is obviously in a lot of pain, so without a second to wait I tell the lady to 'follow me'. The Swansea PDSA PetAid hospital is fortunately only a minute away and I call through on my mobile phone to warn them what is happening. We arrive quickly and I'm greeted by one of the nurses. We rush the dog through to the preparation room and open the dog's mouth. Fortunately the stick has just jammed in the dog's back teeth, so we carefully remove it with a pair of forceps. Sometimes the stick goes all the way down a dog's throat, which can be horrible!

I give the dog an injection of antibiotics, to prevent any infection and the dog is then back to its old self, jumps down off the table and we take him out to his grateful owner.

The receptionist has taken down a few details whilst she was waiting so we now know that the dog is called Duggie. He's a little Jack Russell Terrier with quite a lot of spirit and it's nice to see him running around, even if he is making a lot of noise!

Steve Howard, Senior Veterinary Surgeon at the Swansea PDSA PetAid hospital describes a working day.

Text extract and photo from PDSA's website courtesy of Veterinary Charity PDSA http://secure.pdsa.org.uk/youngpdsa © PDSA

Internet

first person pronoun indicates recount is told by the vet himself

explains who the recount is written by, and what it's about

capital letters for names

1: 3: T18: to read recounts and begin to recognise generic structure

1: 3: T20: to write simple recounts linked to topics of interest/study or to personal experience

Trip to the park

illustrated by Simon Rumble

Background

Recount writing is organised chronologically and can be used, for example, to describe events in history, give an account of something which has happened, provide a biography (see 'Diary of a PDSA vet', for example, which can be seen as recounting an event and as an autobiographical extract). It can take the form of writing in sentences, but can also be presented in other formats such as timelines and flow charts. This is the first of a series of three lessons which looks at different types of recount, this one based on the theme of a visit to the park. This text takes the form of a 'comic strip', where events are told through pictures. In the second and third texts the style of presentation changes to a timeline and then to a flow chart. The illustrations here provide a structure for shared writing of a chronological account.

What's on the CD-ROM

The differentiated text repeats the pictures from the core text, but provides sentence prompts which include time connectives to scaffold the language of recounts.

Discussing the text

● Explain to the children that you are going to be looking at a story which is told through pictures. Look at the sequence of pictures and ask the children to discuss with their think, pair and share partners what they can see in each picture. Confirm the context of the story, and ask the children to point out details in the illustrations. List key words on the board, modelling how to spell them by segmenting and blending as you write.

● Next, ask the children to look at the first picture and to tell you what is happening in it. Ask for suggestions of an opening sentence for an account of the visit to the park which describes what they can see in the picture. They should imagine that the children in the picture are from their class. Remind them that the sentence should explain who went, where they went, and when it happened (they will need to make this up). Agree on a sentence and scribe it under the picture, emphasising the *when*, *who* and *where* as you are writing.

● Move on to the second picture and introduce a word or phrase which indicates time, such as *First...* or *The first thing we saw...* Ask for suggestions for the rest of the sentence.

● For the third picture, split the class into two groups, with one going to the *Lake* and one to the *Aviary.* Begin a sentence for each with another word or phrase which indicates a change of time such as *Next*, *After that* or *When*.

● Continue to look at the pictures and to write sentences for all but two or three, explaining to the children that they will be able to use the pictures and the list of key words on the differentiated version of the text to help them to write their own sentences for these.

Talk, read and write

● Ask confident writers to write sentences independently or in pairs about the remaining pictures. For others, use the differentiated text and read the incomplete sentences with them, asking them to suggest what they might say. Do this orally, but ask the children to refer to the word list to match their oral suggestions with written words. Once you have finished scribing sentences for the remaining pictures, ask the children to recount the story of the visit once more, using the pictures as prompts.

Extension

If possible, take children to a nearby park and help them to write a recount of their visit.

Ask the children to research different parks. There are many useful websites about parks, including www.terragalleria.com/pictures-subjects/urban-parks, which contains pictures of urban parks from around the world which could be used as prompts for discussions and comparisons with local parks.

In design and technology work, children could design parks and label them, drawing on the vocabulary introduced in this lesson.

Create a display of park pictures and add cards with key vocabulary to label it. The display can then be added to in future lessons and can act as a wordbank for children working independently.

pictures organised in clear chronological sequence

1: 3: T20: to write simple recounts linked to topics of interest/study or to personal experience

encourage children to include some descriptive information, eg: 'the flowers smelled lovely'

ask children to include information about 'how?' in opening paragraph, eg: 'Our teacher made us promise to behave ourselves – otherwise we would have to go back to school.'

clear opening event which establishes who, where, what

1: 3: T18: to read recounts and begin to recognise generic structure

clear closing event. Ensure language of recount reflects this through phrases such as 'Finally'; 'It was getting late so…'; 'It was time…'

1: 3: S6: through reading and writing, to reinforce knowledge of term *sentence* from previous terms

1: 3: W8: to learn new words from reading and shared experiences

Illustrations © Simon Rumble/Beehive Illustration

Kylie's life

by David Waugh

Background

This text provides a simple timeline for a child's life from birth to age 6, which can be discussed and modified and tailored to individual pupils. The lesson builds on the previous one in which a recount was produced for a visit to the park. Some of the vocabulary listed for that lesson can be used again for this one, particularly that to do with time and sequence, as can the sequenced pictures. By exploring this text, the children look at an alternative method of presenting information about events in chronological order – a timeline. Before attempting to reproduce the information about the park visit as a timeline, show the children a few examples of timelines in addition to this one. The activities can be linked to work in maths on processing, representing and interpreting data, and to chronological understanding in history. This timeline can also be linked to the text 'Dear Tom' on page 108. In preparation for this lesson, ask the children to try to find out dates for key events in their lives such as their birthday, taking their first steps, first words spoken, starting nursery and starting school.

What's on the CD-ROM

The CD-ROM contains a partially completed timeline for the visit to the park, drawing on the sequence of events from the previous lesson. This can be used to start the children off in compiling their own timelines of the visit. You might want to adapt this text if you have taken the class to a park following the previous lesson.

Discussing the text

● Present the timeline and discuss what it is about. Then, to prompt examination of the details, ask the children questions such as: *Where does the timeline start: from the left or from the right? Which is the first/second/ third... event shown? Which is the final event shown?* Ensure that children understand that the arrow represents the passing of time (and the direction), and that events are set out in the order in which they occurred.

● Draw a timeline on the board and ask a child to help you to complete it with events from his or her life so far. Compare this child's 'key milestones' with Kylie's. What other important events might be included on a child's timeline?

● Highlight the abbreviation *b.* for *born* and talk with the children about other abbreviations they may know such as PC, RE and PE. Explain that abbreviations that represent several words almost always have capital letters.

● Next, remind the children of the previous lesson and look at the partially completed timeline from the differentiated text on the CD-ROM. Read it to and with the children. Discuss the order of events and ask the children to suggest which additional events should be inserted into the spaces. Check the sequence of events by revisiting the text from the previous lesson.

Talk, read and write

● Ask some children to work independently in pairs to complete the timeline of the visit to the park, using copies of the text from the previous lesson to help them. Provide the most able learners with a blank timeline and ask them to use their own words to complete it.

● Guide other children as they complete the timeline by asking them to suggest what might be written in each section, and then modelling this on the board or individual whiteboards before they attempt to write. Encourage the children to modify what you have written and to use their own words wherever possible. Look carefully at the words which you and the children use and draw attention to common spelling patterns. Reinforce children's understanding by asking them for other words with the same patterns. Write these on the board and discuss how the graphemes relate to the phonemes.

Extension

Encourage children to look in the class and/or school library for further examples of timelines, especially from history texts, and make a display of these.

Ask children to talk with family members (from different generations if possible) about significant events in their lives and to work with adults to produce timelines which can be brought into school to add to the display.

1: 3: T18: to read recounts and begin to recognise generic structure

1: 3: T17: to recognise that non-fiction books on similar themes can give different information and present similar information in different ways

a visual form of recount

events on a timeline can be represented by pictures or words

1: 3: T20: to write simple recounts linked to topics of interest/study or to personal experience

details key events which are typical of a young child's life

1: 3: T21: to use the language and features of non-fiction texts

1: 3: S5: to know other common uses of capitalisation, such as for personal titles, headings, book titles, emphasis

tense changes to present for final entry as this is 'now'

gaps between events are all the same though time periods vary – timeline is diagrammatic only

timeline starts with Kylie's birth. Note b. for 'birth'

Kylie's Life: Here is a (timeline) of Kylie's first six years.

5 months old. Kylie's first tooth came through.

In January 2002 Kylie started going to nursery school.

Kylie was 4 when she started school in September 2004.

Kylie walker b. 23 September 1999

At 13 months, Kylie started to walk. She also said her first word.

Kylie stopped wearing nappies. She was 3 years old

6 June 2006: Kylie is 6 years old. She is in Y1

Text © 2007, David Waugh; photos © 2006, Jupiter Images Corporation

Making toast

by David Waugh

Background
This text is the third in the series looking at chronological recounts presented in different ways. In this final lesson, a recount text is presented as a flow chart with each event appearing in a separate box linked by arrows. The commentary describing the events is brief and not necessarily in complete sentences. The text will provide useful experience of flow charts for use in science.

What's on the CD-ROM
The differentiated text provided on the CD-ROM is set out as a blank flow chart. It can be used either to add in details of the visit to the park or to scaffold talking and writing about other events.

Discussing the text
● Begin by asking the children if any of them have ever made toast (point out that they should only ever do this when supervised by an adult). When do they make it and what equipment do they use? What toppings do they enjoy? In pairs, allow the children first to talk through the process with each other, and then ask for volunteers to demonstrate how they would make it, using actions and words.

● Look at the sample flow chart and read it to and with the children. Experiment with rearranging the order of the text and ask the children to suggest how it should be ordered. Manipulate the text so that it is in the order the children suggest. Read it with them again to check that it is correct.

● Address some of the features of a flow chart, for example that it is sequential; there is no need for words like *first, next* and *finally* because the order is implicit; arrows can be used to show the direction of the process or the sequence of events. Compare the flow chart with the timeline from the previous lesson and discuss why you might use one or the other. (A timeline is more suitable for marking events over a long period of time, whereas a flow chart is often used to explain a process.)

Talk, read and write
● Show the children the blank flow chart from the CD-ROM and remind them about the work on the park visit. If necessary, return to the timeline or the picture-based recount to recap on events.

● Model how to capture the first two events in note style (*Went into park*; *Looked at flowers*.) Emphasise the way in which the flow chart text is presented in short clauses rather than sentences. A flow chart can contain full sentences, but often we leave out personal pronouns and determiners (*the, a* and so on) to keep it concise.

● Invite the children to suggest what events from the park visit should be written in the third box in the flow chart and then the fourth. Check the spellings of the words they choose. If you have begun a display about parks, point out some of the words which children suggest and remind them that they can look at the display to help them with spellings. If they do this, encourage them to look carefully at the word they need, say it, write it down without looking at it, then check to see if they have written it correctly.

● Ask the most able learners to attempt to complete the blank flow chart independently, but encourage them to draw upon the word list and, if you have made one, the display of words and pictures related to parks.

● Work with the other children as they use the vocabulary to continue and complete the flow chart. Ask about how they think you could show that two groups did different things at the same time (visiting the lake and the aviary). At this point, for example, the chart could split and then the two branches could rejoin when the children came together again as a class for a picnic.

Extension
Children could make their own flow charts for different activities or processes, including getting ready for school, getting ready for playtime, cleaning teeth, making chocolate crunchies or growing a plant from a seed. For the last example, you could refer to the cycle for growing a sunflower from Term 1 (page 40) and could discuss the differences between cycle diagrams and flow charts.

Text © 2007, David Waugh

1: 3: T21: to use the language and features of non-fiction texts

past tense verbs

the arrow points to the next box to reinforce the linear sequencing of events

1: 3: S6: through reading and writing, to reinforce knowledge of term sentence from previous terms

MAKING TOAST

We **took** a slice of bread out of the packet.

We **put** the bread into the toaster.

We **set** the toaster to the right number. The higher the number, the darker your toast is.

While the bread was toasting, we got out a plate, a knife and some butter to spread on the toast.

When the toast popped up, we left it for a short time so that it didn't burn our fingers.

We spread some butter on the toast – and then we ate it!

first person plural; tells the reader that there were several people who took part in this event

each step is set out in a different box

events are set out in chronological order

clear, straightforward use of language allows reader to follow the chain of events

connectives indicating time help to link the events together

1: 3: T17: to recognise that non-fiction books on similar themes can give different information and present similar information in different ways

1: 3: W7: to spell common irregular words from Appendix List 1

A school trip to the seaside

by David Waugh

Background

This recount consists of a sequence of pictures related to a trip to the seaside, accompanied by text in which the children on the trip describe what they did or saw. The text is a chronological recount of the day, beginning and ending with the coach journeys there and back. To help in setting the scene and establishing the context, display pictures of the seaside and/or show a video clip to remind children what the seaside is like. The activity can be linked to other work on personal recounts, such as 'Trip to the park' (page 92) and 'The day I brought my first pet home' (page 86), and can be used to reinforce the language of recounts. It can also be linked to work in geography on knowledge and understanding of places.

What's on the CD-ROM

This version repeats the six pictures from the core text, but omits the accompanying text. This enables it to be used to support oral and written recounts. A selection of time connectives are included along the bottom of the page to support the use of sequential language.

Discussing the text

● Mask the words on the text, so that you begin by looking at the pictures and the title only. Ask the children what they expect the text will tell them. Share experiences of the seaside, asking the children what they know and what they have done when/if they been there.

● Working in pairs, ask the children to describe what they can see in each picture. Encourage them to rehearse sentences that could be used in a recount by using the first person, past tense.

● Take feedback on the first picture and write up key words which may be useful in forming sentences, for example *coach/bus, driver, depart, leave, seat, seat belt, beach, sea*. Talk about the words and their spellings, focusing in particular on the long vowel phoneme 'ee' which is a feature of several of the words.

● Next, write on the board a sentence suggested by one pair of children and ask the rest of the class to suggest how it could be modified, by changing the phrasing or adding more information, or both. Go on to do the same for two or three more of the pictures, ensuring that initial sentences begin with a word which indicates a change of time and a sequence of events.

● As you write with the children, emphasise the need for capital letters and full stops and talk about the need to ensure that sentences make sense. Reinforce this by leaving some sentences incomplete and asking the children what will be needed to complete them so that they make sense.

● Finally, reveal the text and read it with the children, comparing it with the version you have created as a class. Ask the children to point out the time words that connect the sections together.

● Discuss how the text could be organised under headings, for example *The journey there; Arriving.*

Talk, read and write

● Look at the differentiated text with the children and read the list of connectives at the bottom of the sheet. Ensure that the list of key words you created earlier is still displayed on the board. Ask pairs of children to use the pictures to retell the sequence of events again. Allow more competent writers to write down some simple sentences individually or in pairs. Work with less able learners to create a simple version of the recount. Alternatively, you could provide some simple cloze sentences for the children to complete.

● An alternative activity could involve providing children with versions of the core or differentiated text cut into sections, for children to re-sequence.

Extension

Ask children to produce storyboards or cartoon strips with brief accompanying text to recount outings with parents and carers. These could include visits to the shops, cinema, museums and so on.

Some children could look at simple non-fiction texts and make collections of words which have the long vowel sound spelled 'ea' and 'ee'. This could lead to discussions about the 'ea' grapheme and its different phonemes, such as in *bread, break, idea* and *wear.*

Text © 2007, David Waugh; photos: clipboard © 2006, Jupiter Images Corporation, blue coach (top right) © Bjarne Kvaale, cliffs © Tiago Pontes, big wheel © Martin Walls, girl on beach © Luc Sesselle, seaweed © Kevin Mark Wood, yellow coach (bottom left) © Ben Oates

1: 3: T20: to write simple recounts linked to topics of interest/study or to personal experience

time connective introduces the second event

describes what they could see and hear

all contain long 'ee' vowel phoneme

final concluding sentence closes the recount

1: 3: S6: through reading and writing, to reinforce knowledge of term *sentence* from pervious terms

A SCHOOL TRIP TO THE SEASIDE

Our trip to the seaside began at 9 o'clock on Monday morning when we set off from the school by bus. We were not allowed to eat on the coach, but the teachers said we could sing.

When we reached the seaside we could see the cliffs from the coach. The waves were crashing. There were seagulls everywhere and they were very noisy.

The coach parked and we walked to the beach. We could see the bright lights of the amusement arcades. At the fair there was a big wheel.

On the beach we found shells and stones. We paddled in the sea and ate our picnic.

In the afternoon we looked in rock pools. We found lots of tiny creatures.

Finally, the coach driver brought the coach back and we set off home.

1: 3: T18: to read recounts and begin to recognise generic structure

title tells you what the text is about

told in first person

first sentence tells you when/where/what the recount is about

all contain long 'ee' vowel phoneme

uses photos to illustrate and structure the recount; similar to photo album approach/presentation

a variety of sentence starters to keep writing varied and interesting

1: 3: W1: to know the common spelling patterns for each of the long vowel phonemes 'ee', 'ai', 'ie', 'oa', 'oo'

KWL grid: owls

by Claire Head

Background

A KWL grid helps children to interact with information from different sources. The K column activates children's *knowledge*; the W column (*what*) establishes the purpose of the investigation by targeted questioning; the L column reflects the outcome of children's research by summarising what has been *learned*. Once children have been introduced to KWL grids they can be used across the curriculum. This text works best when used in conjunction with the non-chronological report 'Owls', which follows this text. KWL grids are one of the strategies recommended as a result of research by the EXEL (Exeter Extending Literacy) project in 1992. This research is explained in *Extending Literacy* by: D Wray and M Lewis. The EXIT model (Extending Interactions with Texts), which explains a range of teaching and learning strategies, is now an integral part of the National Literacy Strategy. To find out more about KWL grids and the EXIT model visit: www.warwick.ac.uk/staff/D.J.Wray/exel/info.html.

What's on the CD-ROM

The alternative version of the text omits the 'How' column. This reduces the reading demands and presents the information as questions and answers. The content of any of the columns can be masked for the purposes of interacting and engaging with the content. For example, delete the *W* column and ask children to help you to write the questions based on the statements in the *K* column.

Discussing the text

● Before showing the class the KWL grid ask them to tell each other in pairs what they know about owls. Take feedback and then reveal the K column of the grid. Explain that the children who made these responses did the same thing. Next, read the introductory section which explains the purpose of the grid.

● Compare the children's answers with those on the grid. Point out any similarities and differences. Explain that at this point this information is what we *think* we know, but we are not sure if they are facts.

● Talk about the differences between fact, fiction and opinion. Some children might have drawn their 'facts' about owls from story books or films. Then discuss how some people know more than others about specific subjects. This is a good opportunity to give positive emphasis to our different strengths and interests. Using a KWL grid is a good method of helping people to work together to share information and to learn more.

● Show the children the next column and explain that this is where the class recorded the questions that they wanted to find answers to. Point out how most of the questions originate from the statements in the K column. Ask the children if they would like to add another question to the list. Model how to write this question by identifying the question word and highlighting the question mark.

Talk, read and write

● During guided group work ask children to think of one more question they can add to the column. You could scaffold this task and provide prompts for different groups by listing the following as potential research areas: hearing, eyesight, hunting, habitat, food, flying, feathers. Once children have completed this task ask each child to read his or her question out to the group. Encourage talk about how they might go about finding the answers. Reveal the *How* column to show how Sally's class answered the questions.

● Work with small groups to explore the final column which reveals what Sally's class learned. Support groups as they rehearse how to ask the question, explain how to research it and then answer it using the information in the grid. Each group can then feed back to the rest of the class.

● Help children to develop a glossary to explain some of the subject-specific words, for example *roost* and *prey*.

Extension

Visit the following websites to learn more about owls: World Owl Trust, www.owls.org/Information/info.htm and World of Owls, www.worldofowls.com.

1: 3: **T22**: to write own questions prior to reading for information and to record answers

1: 3: **S7**: to add question marks to questions

1: 3: **T17**: to recognise that non-fiction books on similar themes can give different information and present similar information in different ways

1: 3: **W8**: to learn new words from reading and shared experiences

the information is linked across the columns. 'Prior knowledge' in column 1 is used as basis for research, leading to an answer in column 4

could also contain diagrams or labelled pictures

provides starting point for creating a report – although information may need to be reorganised into a more logical structure

stands for 'Know', 'What', 'Learned'

contextualises the grid; not part of the template but introduces it

questions formulated using 'what', 'why', 'how', 'when', 'where'

questions could be used as sub-headings in final report

statements in column are organised from general to more specific

---

KWL Grid: OWLS

Hi, my name is Sally. I am in class 1B. My class have just finished a project about owls. We have learned a lot. Here is our KWL grid. It took us three weeks to research the information. The 'How' column in the grid below shows you what we did to learn about owls.

Now we are all owl experts!

Know (What do we think we know about owls?)	What (What do I want to find out about owls?)	How (What did we do to find out the information?)	Learned (What have we learned about owls?)
Owls are birds.	What type of bird?	Looked up 'owl' in a dictionary.	Owls are birds of prey.
Owls come out at night.	Why don't we see owls in the daytime?	Used an information book.	Owls are nocturnal. They hunt at night.
They make a 'too-whit-to-whoo' sound.	Why do owls say 'too-whit-to-whoo'?	Researched on the internet.	They make this sound to call each other.
They eat mice, voles, hedgehogs, grass snakes, young birds, fish, insects, bats, rats and frogs.	How do owls catch their prey?	A speaker from an owl sanctuary told us.	Owls have excellent hearing. They can hear animals moving around. They catch their prey in their sharp talons.

Are you as wise as an owl?

Owls

by Claire Head

Background

This non-chronological report about owls exemplifies many of the traditional features of this genre. The formal style and some of the technical vocabulary will challenge the children but the glossary offers support and the interesting facts will capture children's attention. This text can be used in conjunction with, or as an extension to, 'KWL grid: Owls'. It also can be seen as a development from other texts on birds, on pages 82 and 84.

What's on the CD-ROM

This much simplified and abbreviated version of the text is accompanied by a simple writing frame which can be used to scaffold children's written and oral work in response to questions about the text and the diagram. This frame can also be used as the starting point to help structure other non-chronological reports during shared and guided writing.

Discussing the text

● Before reading, explain to the children that this text is a report about owls and that the author had to find out information about the following questions before writing this text: *What is an owl? What do owls look like? Where do owls live? What do owls eat? What do owls sound like?* Display these questions, read them with the class and highlight the question marks and use of capital letters.

● Give the children a few minutes to think, pair and share in response to each question. Record some of their ideas and answers in note form under each question. Then tell the children that you are going to read the report so that they can learn the facts about owls and find out if their answers to the questions were correct.

● Read the text, pausing to talk about each section. Point out the glossary to help explain unfamiliar words such as *prey* and *nocturnal*. It would be helpful if you could show the class other photographs or film clips of owls at this point. A labelled picture might also be useful.

● Talk about some of the specific action words the author has selected, for example *swoop* and *seize*. It might help to encourage role play for these actions, but ensure the swooping owls are gentle when they seize their victims!

● After reading, ask the children to help you to match the questions to each section of the report. (If you are using an interactive whiteboard you can cut and paste the sentences into position, or write the sentences on long strips of paper so that they can be fixed in place on an enlarged version of the text.) Talk about how the author has organised and grouped the information into collections of sentences about similar things, for example food, habitat and sound.

● Ask the children to tell a friend one new fact that they have learned about owls from reading this text.

Talk, read and write

● Use the writing frame provided with the differentiated version of the text to help children answer questions about the text.

● Ask the children during guided group work to use reference books and websites to find out the names of different types of owls. Ask the children to describe specific owls and draw their own labelled diagrams. The following website is a useful source of pictures and information: http://aviary/owls.com/owls.html.

● Challenge more able learners and those who have become owl experts to find out more interesting facts about owls to be included in a 'Did you know?' display in the classroom. For example, ask: *What are baby owls called?* (Owlets.) *What does 'mobbing' mean?* (When a group of small birds discover a sleeping owl near their nests they fly around it making a lot of noise to drive the owl away.) *What is special about an owl's neck and head?* (It can turn its head round until it is facing almost backwards, giving it all-round vision.)

● Use the original text as a model to help children write their own reports about another animal (perhaps another bird). You could model this during shared writing first by using the questions as subheadings to organise the facts.

Extension

If possible take the children on a visit to an owl sanctuary or invite an expert to visit the school to talk about owls.

1: 3: T21: to use the language and features of non-fiction texts

typical feature of non-fiction information text

classification of information typical of non-chronological report

glossary definitions not complete sentences

the first sentence of each paragraph is the topic sentence – it tells the reader what information the paragraph is going to cover

1: 3: W8: to learn new words from reading and shared experiences

Text © 2007, Claire Head; photos: top © Eszter Szollosi, bottom left © Juha Blomberg, bottom right © Pamela Menn

OWLS

Owls are birds of prey. There are over 170 different species of owls including Barn Owls, Snowy Owls and Tawny Owls.

Owls have round heads, forward-facing eyes and small, pointed beaks. Most owls have soft brown, grey or white feathers.

Owls can be found in every part of the world except in Antarctica. Most owls prefer to live in a woodland habitat.

Owls are mainly nocturnal. They hunt at night using their excellent hearing and eyesight. Owls eat mice, grass snakes, frogs, fish and young birds. They swoop down silently and seize their prey in their sharp talons.

Owls often make a screeching noise. Sometimes you can hear owls calling 'too-whit-to-whoo' to each other.

GLOSSARY

Birds of prey birds that hunt other living things for food

Habitat where a creature lives, it's home

Nocturnal animals that come out at night and sleep in the daytime.

Talons sharp claws

first sentence provides a definition of the subject matter;

describes the typical appearance of owls

technical vocabulary linked to subject

tells the reader where owls can be found (habitat)

formal language; generalised discussion of all owls, not one specific individual

1: 3: T19: to identify simple questions and use text to find answers

1: 3: S7: to add question marks to questions

1: 3: T22: to write own questions prior to reading for information and to record answers

Wrapping it up

by Steve Parker

Background
This report explains how and why certain food packaging is used. This will be a challenging text for most Year 1 children, but practical and familiar resources can be used to help them to engage with the information. It links to science work on sorting and using materials and can also be part of a project on recycling. It can also be used in conjunction with the extracts 'Waste' on page 52 and 'What is a bike made of?' on page 106. If possible, set up a supermarket home corner in which the children can handle, sort and classify different sorts of packaging material. Also gather a selection of different food packages.

What's on the CD-ROM
The differentiated version of the extract focuses on identifying and sorting materials. Children can complete the materials chart provided once they have engaged in some practical work. You could use this text to play a question-and-answer game about materials and their uses.

Discussing the text
● Read the title of the extract to the children and say that it is a clever clue. Ask for ideas on what the text might be about. Reveal the text and explain that it is about food packaging. Read the introductory explanation.
● Point out the question used as a subheading. Highlight the question word *What* and the question mark. Explain that the bulleted list below will provide the answers to this question. There are four bullet points and that means four facts about packaging. After reading and discussing the bullet points, write questions such as the following on the board, pausing for children to think, pair and share after each one: *Why do packages have designs on the outside? What would happen if food wasn't packaged? What do manufacturers do? What is packaging made from?* When children feed back, highlight the part of the text that contained the sought-after information.
● Now focus on the box containing an explanation of how packaging is designed. Point out that there are three stages designers go through, and number each stage. Read stage 1 and ask the children why a cardboard box is used to package fish fingers. After

feedback, read stages 2 and 3 and then ask the children to tell a friend what sort of package their favourite food comes in.
● Next, produce a shopping bag full of packages, such as cardboard boxes, tins, plastic bottles and pots, polystyrene trays. (Ensure empty packages are clean and have no sharp edges.) Tell the children that you want them to guess what sort of food or drink each package contains as you take it from the bag. (You will need to mask brand names and pictures or take off labels where possible.) Ask the children to justify their guesses by explaining what the package is made from.

Talk, read and write
● In guided group work, encourage the children to write their own questions to ask which is the most suitable material to contain specific food items. You could make a game from the alternative text to stimulate this activity. Give one child a card with a food word on it (for example *margarine*; *eggs*; *milk*) and that child has to describe the best material to contain it (plastic carton; cardboard box; glass or plastic bottle). Once children are familiar with this game they can use their knowledge to write simple questions for each other about packaging: *Which food is put in a jar? Which food is put in a bag?*
● Alternatively, create a feely bag in which you have placed different kinds of packaging. Ask the children to place their hand inside the bag, and describe one of the objects. After the other children have worked out what it is, but before it is removed from the bag, encourage them to think what kind of food might have been stored in it.
● Focus on the 'p' phoneme. Identify words in the text beginning with 'p' and talk about initial consonant blends containing 'p', for example *plain* and *protect*.
● Play games with the compound word *cardboard*. Identify vowels and consonants. Find words within the word and use the letters to create new words.

Extension
Children could bring from home one clean, empty food package which they can label and classify as part of a shared display.

title is a play on words: 'wrapping it up' is another way of describing packaging; it's also an expression for a conclusion

1: 3: T19: to identify simple questions and use text to find answers

definition

subject-specific terminology

commas to separate items in a list

question used as a sub-heading

used to organise the information

1: 3: S7: to add question marks to questions

1: 3: W9: to learn the terms 'vowel' and 'consonant'

Wrapping it up

Manufacturers, the people who make things, package most food before it goes to the shops. They put it in boxes and cartons, bags and cans, jars and bottles. Some packaging is made of plastic, some of glass, and some of paper and cardboard.

What is packaging for?

- Packaging helps to protect food and keep it fresh.
- Packaging makes food easy to store in the shops and easy to take home.
- Packaging helps customers to see what they are buying. It gives them information about what is inside.
- Food is packaged in different sizes, so customers can buy the amount they need.

Designers plan how to package food in the best way.

1. Fish fingers would not fit in a bottle or a jar or a can. They might get squashed in a polythene bag.

2. A cardboard box is best. It is the right shape. It will protect the fish fingers. And it is not too heavy.

3. A plain box would look boring, and it would not show what is inside. It needs a design.

Most of the things we buy have packaging for the same reasons.

Text extract and illustrations from "How things are made" by Steve Parker © 1992, Kingfisher Publications plc

starts with the word 'packaging' to reinforce subject matter. Gives advantages of packaging, and the benefits to shoppers

shows visual examples of packaging

uses 'fish fingers' as an example to explain the process of choosing the right kind of packaging

1: 3: T22: to write own questions prior to reading for information and to record answers

begins by explaining why certain types of packaging would not be suitable

goes on to show why a certain type of packaging is suitable

describes why the packaging needs to have a design

1: 3: S6: through reading and writing, to reinforce knowledge of term *sentence* from previous terms

final paragraph links specific example to generalised point about all products

What is a bike made of?

by Steve Parker

Background

This extract, from the same book (*How things are made*) as the previous text, is presented as a large labelled photograph of a bicycle. The labels include mention of what the different parts of the bicycle is made of. Talking about this familiar object will interest most children, and can be linked to science topic work on materials and their properties. If you can, bring in a real bike as the starting point for activities based on this text.

What's on the CD-ROM

The differentiated version of the text has a grid using questions on the 'materials and their properties' aspect of a bicycle. This can be used to scaffold class, group or individual activities.

Discussing the text

● Hide the bicycle if you have one available. Make a set of flashcards from the names of the bicycle parts labelled (in bold). Tell the children to listen carefully as you read out some of the flashcard labels as this will give them some clues about the object (a bicycle) that you have hidden from view.

● Begin with some of the less familiar words, for example *hub, fork, frame* and then continue by including more recognisable clues: *tyre, handlebar, spoke, chain*. Ask the children to whisper to a friend as soon as they have worked out what the mystery object is and then put their hands up to feed back.

● Wheel in or reveal the bike that you had hidden and congratulate correct guessers. Tell the children that with their help you will be able to match all of the labels to the correct parts of the bike.

● First, ask the children which parts of the bike they can identify (pointing to the particular parts as necessary). Use their answers to begin the labelling process. Attach each label in turn to the bike (pegs or string should work) and as each label finds a home, ask the class to consider what each part of the bike is made from. Encourage children to assign all the labels even if they have to guess the correct place for some.

● Once this process has been completed, ask the children to tell you how they could find out if their labelling and talking has been accurate.

If, for example, they have said that some parts of the bike are made of metal – what sort of metal?

● Finally, show the children the extract and explain that you can use this information text to check your labels and to learn some special words related to bicycles and the parts that make them up.

Talk, read and write

● Ask the children to spot the question on the page and then read the title together. Elicit that *bike* is a shortened form of the word *bicycle*.

● Read each label and follow the key line to the picture, and involve the children in checking that the labels on the real bike are in a similar place. Point out that the labels are in bold and the extra information tells the reader what material each labelled part is made from.

● Ask individuals to feel specific parts of the bike and to tell you more about its properties, for example *It feels hard/soft/bendy/bumpy/smooth/cold…* Use the table provided on the differentiated text to support children when describing properties.

● Consider why specific materials have been used where they have, for example rubber for the tyres and the handlebar grip. Identify the different types of metal that have been named on the diagram.

● Ask the children to use the labelled diagram to locate answers to specific questions about the bike. For example, *Rubber is used in two places on this bike, can you name them?* More able learners could be challenged to write their own questions for the class.

● Ask the children to draw and label your bike or their own bike. Encourage them to use the flashcards as a wordbank.

Extension

Challenge children to identify other things around their homes made from metal – particularly steel (which can be tested with a magnet) and aluminium, plastic or rubber.

1: 3: T21: to use the language and features of non-fiction texts

1: 3: W8: to learn new words from reading and shared experiences

compound word

several 'brake' components

technical information linked to type of material used and topic

definition

general introduction

The parts come from factories in several countries around the world.

title in the form of a question

handlebar/grip rubber

brake lever steel

brake cable steel covered in nylon

fork chromoly

hub aluminium

frame a metal called chromoly – a type of steel

What is a bike made of?

A bicycle has hundreds of parts, made of all sorts of materials.

The **saddle** is made of plastic, with foam padding for comfort and a vinyl cover.

spoke steel

wheel rim aluminium

photograph of a bike rather than a drawing as detail is important

shortened form of word

explanation

bold labels indicate parts

additional text explains material part is made of

brake caliper aluminium

chain steel

valve steel and brass

tyre rubber

valve cap plastic

Text extract and illustrations from "How things are made" by Steve Parker © 1992, Kingfisher Publications plc

1: 3: T19: to identify simple questions and use text to find answers

1: 3: S7: to add question marks to questions

1: 3: T22: to write own questions prior to reading for information and to record answers

Dear Tom

by Claire Head

Background

This activity is based upon a letter from a child in India to a pen pal in the UK, recounting a day at school. The text is an informal letter which includes a timetable for a day's lessons. There are Indian names which can all be read by breaking them down phonically. This will provide an opportunity for children to apply their growing phonic knowledge to unfamiliar words and to segment and blend phonemes. This text can be linked to work in mathematics (processing, representing and interpreting data) and geography (geographical enquiry and skills, and knowledge and understanding of places) and offers useful practise of reading and writing informal letters and emails.

What's on the CD-ROM

The differentiated text provided on the CD-ROM is a simplified version of the letter with a more straightforward timetable than the original. The timetable is presented in a single column, allowing the adjacent column to be used to compare a British timetable with the Indian timetable. The activity can be linked to work on timelines in 'Kylie's life' (page 94).

Discussing the text

● Show the children the text and explain that it is a letter from India. The sender, Sunil, is nine-years-old and he and his pen-friend, Tom, who lives in England, write to each other regularly. Draw the children's attention to the sender's address and explain that the names are unfamiliar (to most of us at least) because they are in India, but that we can read them because we know the sounds they are made up of. Demonstrate by reading one of the names segment by segment.

● Read the letter to and then with the children. Talk about the timetable and the subjects which the children are familiar with as well as those which they might not have heard of, such as *Malayalam* and *Hindi*. Look at the words and show how they can be read by segmenting the sounds: *Mal-ay-al-am* and *Hin-di*. Talk about English words which have similar sounds within them. For example, for *Malayalam*: *say, way, day*; *pal, ham, jam*. Point out the capital letters at the beginning of the words, indicating names. Explain that

Malayalam is a language spoken by around 25 million people in the state of Kerala in southern India. *Hindi* is one of the official languages of India and is the most widely spoken language in the country, with more than 200 million people using it as a first or second language. Children might be interested to know that Sunil learns three languages in his school!

● Look at some of the other Indian words and ask the children to discuss in pairs how they might be pronounced, before sharing their ideas with the class. If you have Malayalam or Hindi speakers in the class, take advantage of their experience!

Talk, read and write

● Look at the differentiated text with children and ask them to compare what Sunil's class does during the day with what they do. Use the blank column to write, with the children's help, the timetable for a typical day for your class. Talk about the spellings of the subjects and ask the children to learn these using Look-Say-Cover-Write-Check. Notice that the Indian school day starts earlier than a typical British school day and ask the children to suggest what might be written in the boxes with times outside the British school day.

● Write a similar letter as a shared writing activity. This letter could be sent to a class in a different country or a different school. Perhaps it could be emailed to a link school in another country.

● Help the children to find out about timetables for other classes in their school, especially Year 2, which they will be entering next year.

Extension

Ask children to talk with older relatives about the school days they remember, and encourage them to bring in written examples for display.

If older classes have links with schools abroad, for example through modern foreign languages studies, ask them to write to their link children to find out about their timetables and then share the results with Year 1.

1: 3: W1: to know the common spelling patterns for each of the long vowel phonemes 'ee' 'ai' 'ie' 'oa' 'oo'

sendee's address set out on the right hand side of the page

situated on the Malabar Coast of southwest India

one of the official languages of India; it is the most widely spoken language in the country

timetable tabulated to make information clear and easy-to-see at a glance; note timetable is for Thursday, the day on which the letter was written

a language spoken by around 25 million people in the state of Kerala in southern India

1: 3: S5: to know other common uses of capitalisation, such as for personal titles, headings, book titles, emphasis

15 Calicut Road
Badagara
Kerala
India

Thursday, 17 June

Dear Tom,

Thank you for your letter. I enjoyed reading about what you do at school. My school is near to my house so it takes me ten minutes to walk there. Do you walk to school every day?

This is what happened at my school today:

My favourite lesson is Geography because we learn about different countries. What's your favourite lesson at school? At play time I like to play football with my friends. What do you play?

From

Sunil

My timetable	Thursday
8.00-8.40	Assembly
8.40-9.15	Hindi
9.15-9.30	Play time
9.30-10.30	English
10.30-11.30	Maths
11.30-12.30	Lunch
12.30-1.00	Geography
1.00-1.30	Malayalam
1.30-1.45	Play time
1.45-2.15	Games
2.15-2.45	Singing

1: 3: T19: to identify simple questions and use text to find answers

date that the letter was written

typical opening of an informal letter; mentions previous correspondence; shows interest in the recipient's life

final paragraph tells recipient about personal preferences and invites a response by asking questions

1: 3: W8: to learn new words from reading and shared experiences

SIGNS GIVING ORDERS

No motor vehicles

No cycling

No towed caravans

Stop and give way

School crossing patrol

WARNING SIGNS

School crossing patrol ahead

Pedestrian crossing

Cycle route ahead

Level crossing without barrier or gate ahead

Low flying aircraft or sudden aircraft noise

Cattle

Walkers' map

If you go walking in the countryside you need a map to help you find your way. What can you see on this walkers' map?

Use the symbols and words at the side of the map to help you follow the walkers' trail. This is called a key and all maps have one.

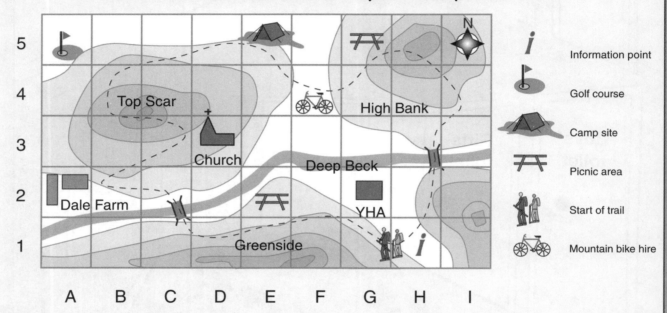

i	Information point
	Golf course
	Camp site
	Picnic area
	Start of trail
	Mountain bike hire

Sometimes, when you are out in the countryside, you see signs like these:

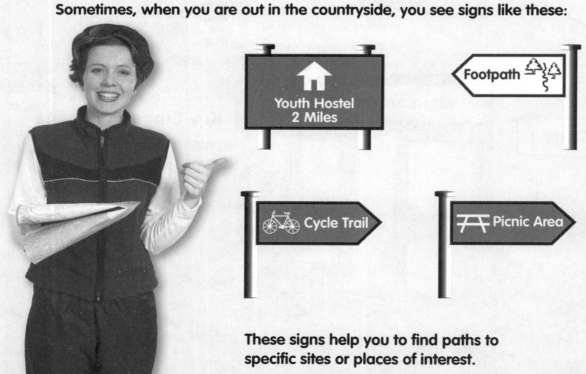

Youth Hostel 2 Miles

Footpath

Cycle Trail

Picnic Area

These signs help you to find paths to specific sites or places of interest.

Text © 2007, Claire Head; photos © 2006, Jupiter Images Corporation

50 Shared texts Non-fiction ● **Year 1**

FANTASTIC OFFERS ON GARDEN TOOLS!

GREEN FINGERS GARDEN CENTRE

LOOK AT THESE PRICES!

RAKE	£5	WATERING CAN	£12	SPADE	£6
SHEARS	£15	GRASS RAKE	£7	FORK	£6
WHEEL BARROW	£50	HOSE PIPE	£10	LAWN MOWER	£100

Leaves

COMPARE DIFFERENT LEAVES

Collect as many different leaves as you can –
deciduous, evergreen, simple and compound. A leaf
with one blade – the flat, green part – is a simple leaf. A
compound leaf, such as horse chestnut leaf, is
made up of several blades. Pine needles are very
thin leaves with a tough wax coat that can
survive cold winters.

**Deciduous
trees have big
green leaves that
collect sunlight in
spring and summer.
In the autumn when
it gets colder, the
leaves fall and die.
Evergreen trees keep
their leaves all
year round.**

pine

horse chestnut

oak

holly

maple

laurel

*Try
making
some leaf
rubbings. Lay white
paper over a leaf
with its underside
facing upwards. Rub the
paper evenly with
a wax crayon and see
the leaf shape and
its raised pattern
of veins
appear.*

Put the leaves in a shoe box and
shut the lid. Check them every few
days. Do all the leaves dry out and
crumble? Do any become 'skeleton'
leaves, when all that is left is the
veins? Do the evergreen leaves
survive the longest?

Text extract from "Plants (Fascinating Science Series)" by Sally Hewitt © 2001, Aladdin Books Ltd (2001, Franklin Watts); photos: background leaves © Penelope Berger, pine leaf © Filip George, horse chestnut leaf © Philip Mamat, oak leaf © Ian Labardee, maple leaf © Chris Root, laurel leaf © Fernando Sanz, holly leaf © Go Vicinity

Term 1: Signs, labels, captions

Flowering plants

Flowering plants grow towards the sun. Light from the sun helps plants to make food. The roots of the plant suck up water and minerals found in the soil. The roots also help to hold the plant firmly in the ground.

What do plants need to live and grow?

Plants need air, sunlight, water and soil to help them grow.

There are all kinds of flowering plants in different colours, shapes and sizes.

Glossary

Leaves – plants spread out their green leaves to catch sunlight to give the plant energy to grow and live.

Petal – colourful scented petals attract insects and birds to the flower.

Roots – these grow down into the soil and suck up water and food.

Soil – this contains water and nutrients for the plant. Dead leaves, rotting plants and insects enrich the soil.

Stem – this is a thin tube that supports the plant and allows water and minerals to travel up to the leaves and petals.

Do you know the names of any flowering plants?

Text © 2007, Claire Head; photos: top left © Maarten Uilenbroek, top right © Lynne Lancaster, centre left © Edwin P, centre right © Ali Taylor, bottom left © Reginaldo Andrade, bottom right © Viktor Hujer

CHRISTMAS IN EUROPE

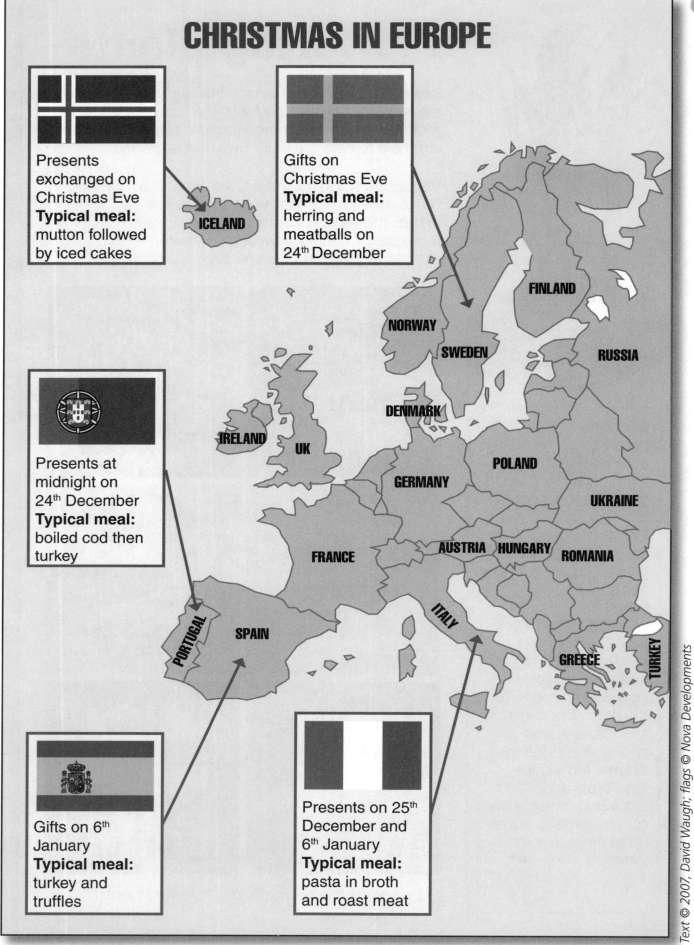

Presents exchanged on Christmas Eve
Typical meal: mutton followed by iced cakes

Gifts on Christmas Eve
Typical meal: herring and meatballs on 24th December

Presents at midnight on 24th December
Typical meal: boiled cod then turkey

Gifts on 6th January
Typical meal: turkey and truffles

Presents on 25th December and 6th January
Typical meal: pasta in broth and roast meat

ICELAND
FINLAND
NORWAY
SWEDEN
RUSSIA
DENMARK
IRELAND
UK
POLAND
UKRAINE
GERMANY
FRANCE
AUSTRIA
HUNGARY
ROMANIA
PORTUGAL
SPAIN
ITALY
GREECE
TURKEY

Text © 2007, David Waugh; flags © Nova Developments

Anita Ganeri/BBC Education; photos © 2006, Derek Cocknell Photography; illustration by The Drawing Room
Text from "Find out about the body" by Anita Ganeri © 1994,

How do we move?

Can you feel hard, knobbly things under your skin? These are your bones. They are strong and hard and hold up your body. You have lots of bones, joined together to make up your skeleton. Without bones, you would flop like jelly.

Rubbery muscles are attached to your bones. Your bones and muscles work together when you move. You use your muscles when you walk, talk, run or play games.

Can you feel the muscles in your arms and legs?

You also use **muscles** to smile and make faces.

the **bones** of the **skeleton** are shown in yellow

can you feel this **muscle** when you **bend** your arm?

rib bone

hip bone

thigh bone

your **backbone** is made up of lots of smaller bones

can you feel your **knee cap?**

the **muscle** at the **back** of your **thigh shortens** when you **bend** your leg

Clothes

We wear different sorts of clothes for different purposes. Some clothes help to keep us warm by trapping heat, made by our bodies, next to the skin.

Clothes we choose to wear when it is warm and sunny are light on the skin and help to keep us cool.

Sometimes we need to wear special clothing that protects us. Can you think of any reasons why someone might need to dress in protective clothing?

It is important to choose the right kind of clothing to wear for everything you do in every kind of weather! Can you help these children choose the best clothes to wear?

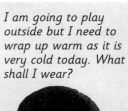

I am going to play outside but I need to wrap up warm as it is very cold today. What shall I wear?

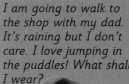

I am going to walk to the shop with my dad. It's raining but I don't care. I love jumping in the puddles! What shall I wear?

I am going on holiday. It will be sunny and hot. I can't wait to go swimming! What shall I take with me to wear?

I am going to ride my bike to my friend's house. I need to make sure I stay safe. What shall I wear?

Text © 2007, Claire Head; photos © 2006, Jupiter Images Corporation

FRUIT

What is a fruit?

A fruit is the fleshy part of a plant that contains its seeds.
It can be eaten. All fruits should be washed before you eat them.
Some fruits need to be peeled before you eat them.

All kinds of fruits

Tropical and exotic fruits

These grow best in hot countries.

**Banana
Mango
Papaya
Pineapple**

Tree fruits

Some of these fruits contain stones in the middle. Do you know which ones?

**Apple
Apricot
Cherry
Fig
Peach
Pear
Plum**

Berries

These soft fruits grow on plants or small bushes. They have many small seeds.

**Bilberry
Blackberry
Blueberry
Cranberry
Raspberry
Strawberry**

Citrus fruits

Citrus fruits contain pips. These can be planted and some will eventually grow into trees.

**Grapefruit
Lemon
Lime
Orange**

Have you ever eaten fruit salad? Which fruits would you include in a fruit salad?

My Food Diary

Day of the week	Breakfast	Lunch	Tea-time	Snacks
Monday	a bowl of cereal	two tuna and cucumber sandwiches	vegetable curry and rice	
Tuesday	one slice of toast with jam	?	fish pie with roast potatoes and broccoli	
Wednesday	a strawberry yoghurt	salad and chicken in pitta bread pockets	a jacket potato with baked beans	
Thursday	a bowl of cereal	three vegetable samosas	?	
Friday	two slices of toast with peanut butter	pasta with tomatoes, ham and onion	omelette with chips and peas	
Saturday	a boiled egg with toasted soldiers	fruit salad	pizza with tomatoes, cheese and pineapple	
Sunday	three pancakes with maple syrup	roast chicken with mashed potatoes, carrots, and parsnips	banana sandwiches and a yoghurt	

On Thursday I went out for my tea with my Grandma and Granddad. We had fish and chips. I had tomato sauce with mine! This is my favourite food. I had some ice-cream with a cherry on top for pudding. Yum!

Text © 2007, Claire Head; photos © 2006, Jupiter Images Corporation

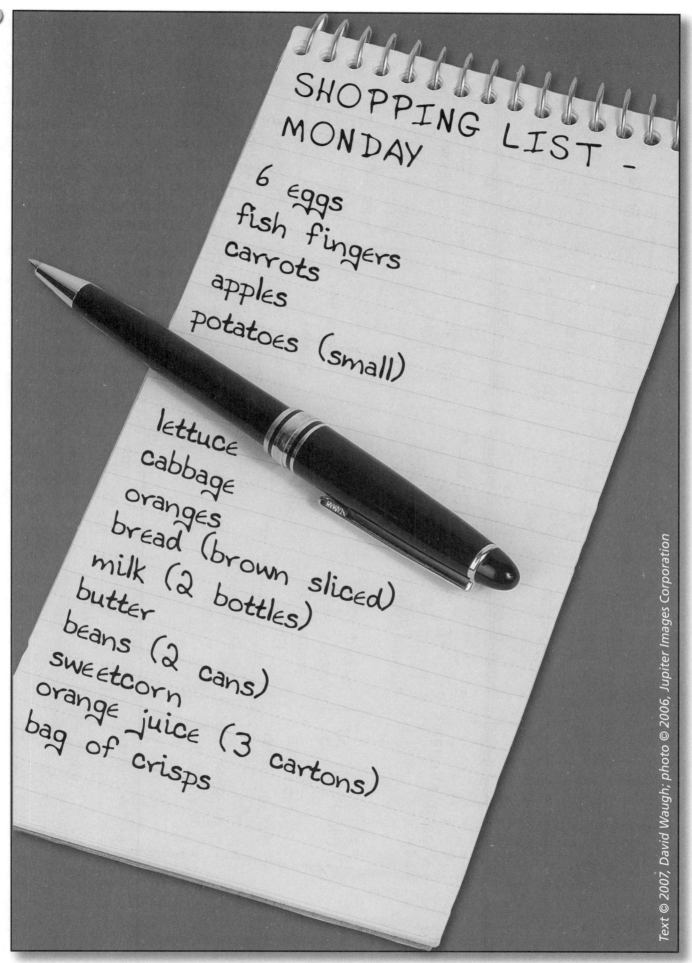

Monday	Tuesday	Wednesday	Thursday	Friday
Roast Turkey *or* Tomato Omelette *or* Vegetable Korma	Chicken Fajitas *or* Jacket Potato and Beans *or* Pasta with Tomato Sauce	Lamb Curry with Rice *or* Jacket Potato and Coleslaw *or* Tuna Wrap	Haddock in Breadcrumbs *or* Cheese Wrap *or* Vegetable Pasta Bake	Sausage Hotpot *or* Bacon and Leek Quiche *or* Vegetable Hotpot
Sweetcorn and Peas Garlic Bread Mixed Salad	Sliced Beans Roast Potatoes Homemade Bread	Mixed Salad Homemade Bread Carrot Batons	Green Cabbage Croquette Potatoes Baked Beans	Chipped Potatoes Peas and Carrots Mixed Salad
Fresh Fruit Salad Yoghurt	Sultana Cookie Yoghurt	Fruit Segments Sultana Scone	Bread and Butter Pudding Apricot Flapjack	Apple Cake and Custard Fresh Fruit
Fruit Juice *or* Water	Fruit Juice *or* Water	Fruit Juice *or* Water	Fruit Juice *or* Water	Fruit Juice *or* Water

Recipe: Fruit Salad

Ingredients
3 bananas
4 apples
5 oranges
1 tin of fruit
cocktail
1 tin of pineapple
chunks
1 bunch of
seedless grapes
1 punnet of
strawberries
½ a lemon

Equipment
2 spoons
1 tin opener
1 large bowl
1 small jug
1 peeler
1 sharp knife
1 colander / sieve
1 large chopping
board

How to make fruit salad

1. Wash the apples, grapes and strawberries.
2. Peel the banana and chop into small chunks. Place in the bowl.
3. Peel the apples and carefully cut into slices. Place in the bowl.
4. Peel the oranges and place segments in the bowl.
5. Pick the grapes and add to the fruit in the bowl.
6. Open the tins of fruit. Drain and save the juice. Pour the fruit into the bowl.
7. Remove the stalks from the strawberries, slice them in half, and place them in the bowl.
8. Pour in some of the saved fruit juice. Squeeze in the juice of half a lemon. Mix everything together gently.
9. Transfer fruit salad into individual dishes and serve. Add one spoonful of ice-cream if desired!

Warning: Be careful when using sharp knives!
Remember to wash your hands before you start preparation.

Text © 2007, Claire Head; photos © 2006, Jupiter Images Corporation

LIGHT FOR LIFE

Green plants need sunlight to live and grow. They use the light's energy to grow. All animals get their food from plants, either directly or indirectly. Since plants need sunlight to grow, all living things depend on the sun.

GROWING CRESS

1. Put a layer of cotton wool in the bottom of two clean dishes. Dampen with a little water. Sprinkle cress seeds evenly over the cotton wool.

2. Put the dishes on a sunny window sill and cover each dish with a cardboard box. Make a hole in the side of one box and leave for several days. Check daily that the cotton wool is damp.

3. The seeds under the box with no hole have grown straight up looking for light. The cress under the box with the hole has grown toward the light.

Text extract and illustrations from "Science for Fun: Light and Colour" by Gary Gibson © 1994, Aladdin Books Ltd (1994, Watts Books)

HARVESTING

We always save some seeds from the
harvested crop for future planting.
We can then grow the same crop next year.

This is the seed-
to-seed cycle of a
sunflower.

1. Seed

7. Plant
decays

2. Seed
begins
to grow

6. Seeds
ripen

3. Plant
grows

5. Seeds begin
to form

4. Flower
appears

A mature sunflower head has a beautiful pattern of seeds
in the centre. If you store some ripe seeds you can
plant them in the spring or give them
to birds in the winter.
We harvest sunflowers for the
oil in their seeds.

Text extract and illustrations from "Autumn" by Susan Humphries © 1986, Macdonald & Co (Publishers) Ltd; photo © Carlos Zaragoza

How to Create an Autumn Leaves Display

RESOURCES

You will need:
A selection of different leaves
Some paint – (red, yellow, brown, green and black)
Paint brushes – (different sizes)
Glue
Twigs
A pencil
Paper
Some felt-tips

PRINTED LEAVES

Follow four easy steps to create an amazing autumn picture.

1. Choose a leaf and select a paint colour.
2. Paint one side of the leaf and then press it down on your sheet of paper.
3. Peel the leaf away carefully. You will see a leaf print left behind.
4. Repeat this action using different leaves and choosing different paint colours.

A FEATHERY OWL

Use the same printing technique to create a fantastic feathery owl picture.

What to do:
First draw the owl's head, eyes and beak at the top of your paper.

Then use small leaves to print the feathers on the owl's body.

Next give your owl two printed feet.

Finally fix a twig along the bottom of your picture so your owl has something to perch on.

Now you are ready to display all your hard work!

Text © 2007, Claire Head; illustrations © Lynne Joesbury; photos © 2006, Jupiter Images Corporation

50 Shared texts Non-fiction ● Year 1

Model toys

Some toys are models of things.
This is a model garage.
It has a car wash and space for cars to park.

Models like like real things.
Can you see what this is a model of?
It is a model farm.

Text © 2007, Scholastic Ltd; photos courtesy of Heritage Play Sets, www.heritageplaysets.com

TOYS THEN AND NOW

Look carefully at these pictures of toys. Are they like the toys you play with? How are they the same? How are they different?

The yo-yo was invented thousands of years ago. The first yo-yos were made out of stone. Later, people carved yo-yos out of wood. What are today's yo-yos made out of?

The first tricycles were built over 160 years ago, long before cars were invented. They were used by adults as a way of getting around – and they were much bigger than the trike you can see here. Who are trikes made for today?

This is a jack-in-the-box. If you turn the handle on the side, it plays a tune. At the end of the tune, the lid opens and a small toy on springs pops out. Why do you think it is called a jack-in-the-box?

People have always made models of everyday things for children to play with. Is this model rocket a modern toy, or is it a toy from the past? How do you know?

Teddy bears come in all sorts of colours, shapes and sizes. How old is this bear? The first teddy bears were made over 100 years ago.

Text © 2007, David Waugh; photos © 2006, Jupiter Images Corporation

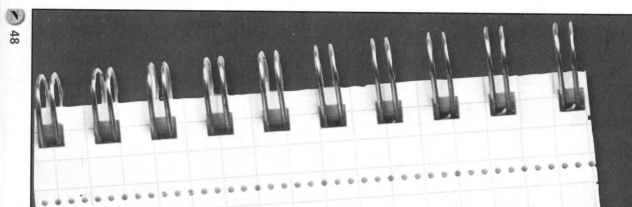

My beautiful doll

When I was six, my Grandma gave me an old doll of hers for Christmas. I still have her today. Her head, legs and arms are made of painted porcelain, and her body is made of cardboard. Her shoes are black, shiny paint. She is dressed in a silk bonnet tied under the chin. Her skirt is made of linen, trimmed with lace and underneath she wears a cream-coloured combination. Her date of birth is written on the back of her neck. I hardly dared to play with her in case I broke her. I wouldn't let anyone else pick her up because she was too special. Her clothes are faded now and some of her painting is scratched but she is still beautiful to me.

Text © 2007, Scholastic Ltd; photo © 2006, Jupiter Images Corporation

TOUCH

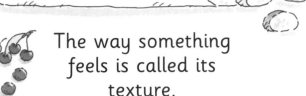

The way something feels is called its texture.
Some things have a different texture on the outside from that on the inside.

like eggs!

You can feel things when you touch them because we have special touch detectors in our skin. These are very small and are hidden in your skin.

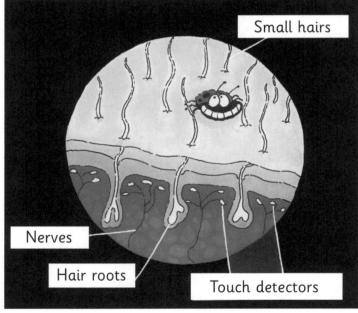

Small hairs

Nerves

Hair roots

Touch detectors

To see the touch detectors you need a very strong microscope.

Text extract and illustrations from "The Senses – Touch" edited by Mandy Suhr © 1993, Wayland (Publishers) Limited

Waste

People in villages, towns, and cities throw away lots of waste.

Recycling

Waste can be sorted. The old paper, glass, and metals are used to make new paper, glass, and metals. This is called recycling.

Getting rid of waste

Most waste is taken away in special lorries. Some waste is tipped into big holes in the ground. Some waste is burned.

There may be special recycling bins where you live. You can leave bottles, cans, and newspapers to be collected for recycling.

Text extract from "Exploring where you live" by Terry Jennings © 1995, Terry Jennings (1995, Oxford University Press); photos: recycle centre © Vicky S, rubbish bins © Denise Hunter

Whether you're completely fearless or a complete scaredy-cat, you need this book. Open it and discover a haunted houseful of spooky surprises packed with fearsome facts, quizzes, stories, games and other things to do.
Find out:

☆ how to trick or treat, carve a pumpkin
and other scary essentials
☆ what to do if you meet a werewolf
☆ some terrifying tales you might believe...
and a few you certainly won't.

Read on and dig up a host of horribly haunting horrors – from A to Z.

Illustrated by Kate Sheppard

A-Z

NON-FICTION

UK **£3.99**

SCHOLASTIC

THE ZONE www.scholastic.co.uk/zone

ISBN 0-439-96326-5

9 780439 963268

Back cover of "The A-Z of ghosts, skeletons and other haunting horrors" by Tracey Turner, illustrated by Kate Sheppard; cover © 2004, Scholastic Children's Books

Index

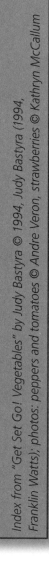

Index from "Get Set Go! Vegetables" by Judy Bastyra © 1994, Judy Bastyra (1994, Franklin Watts); photos: peppers and tomatoes © Andre Veron, strawberries © Kathryn McCallum

HOW DOES A FLOWER GROW?

Bill Bruce

Designed by Mike Edwards
Illustrated by Naz Wasim

Series editor: Helen Parkinson

CONTENTS

Text © 2007, Scholastic Ltd; photo © Louise Docker

Index

CONTENTS

Text © 2007, Scholastic Ltd; photos: contents, top to bottom: © Sarah Joos, Jean Scheijen, Jeff Osborn, Luis Rock; index: top © Valentina Jori, bottom © Jeff Osborn

a b c d e f g h i j k l m n o p q r s t u v w x y z

Different kinds of homes:

Bungalow:
A bungalow is a house built on one level. This means that bungalows don't have stairs inside them.

Caravan:
A caravan is a home on wheels. Most caravans are pulled by cars.

Castle:
A castle is where kings and queens used to live. They were built with big, strong walls to keep people safe during battles.

Detached house:
A detached house is not joined to another house. They are often built in the country, where there is more space.

Flat:
Flats are built one on top of another. They are usually found in cities.

Mobile home:
A mobile home isn't built into the ground. This means that it can be picked up and moved to a new place.

Narrowboat:
A narrowboat is a floating house! People use narrowboats for holidays.

Semi-detached house:
A semi-detached house is joined to another house. They share one wall.

Terraced house:
Terraced houses are joined together in a long row.

Text © 2007, Melissa Mackinlay; photos: castle, detached house, flats, mobile home © IKON Imaging, narrowboat © Simon Gray, terraced house © Giuseppe C

50 Shared texts Non-fiction ● Year 1

Houses and homes

Houses come in all sorts of shapes, sizes and designs. Some are big, some are small. Some are very old and some are new. Here are some pictures of houses and homes:

These are semi-detached houses. Semi-detached houses are joined by one wall.

Terraced houses are built in a long row. These ones have two floors.

Here is a block of flats. Flats are usually built in the middle of cities, where there isn't a lot of space. If you live at the top of a block of flats, you get a very good view of the town down below you.

This bungalow is made out of wood. Bungalows are houses that are all on one level.

Everyone's house is different. What does your home look like?

Text © 2007, Melissa Mackinlay; photos: semi-detached house and flats © IKON Imaging, terraced house © Giuseppe C, bungalow © Lonnie Bradley

Squirrels

The grey squirrel has a grey back, a white underside and a bushy grey tail. They can grow up to 26cm in length. Squirrels are rodents.

Grey squirrels can leap from tree to tree. They cling on to smooth branches with their sharp clawed feet and keep their balance with their long tails. Squirrels can go down tree trunks head first. They are also able to swim.

Squirrels live in dreys. These are nests made of twigs, leaves, grass and moss rolled together in the shape of a football. Squirrels build their nests in holes inside tree trunks or in the fork of a tree.

Squirrels get most of their food from trees. They eat seeds, fruit and nuts. Sometimes they eat insects, flowers, birds' eggs and tree shoots. Squirrels do not hibernate but in winter, they dig up nuts that they have stored underground.

Baby squirrels are born in spring or in summer. The mother cares for her young who are born blind and deaf.

Glossary

Hibernate: some animals sleep through the winter months when there is not as much food available.

Rodents: a type of mammal e.g. rats, mice, voles.

Text © 2007, Claire Head; photo © Stephen Rainer

50 Shared texts Non-fiction ● Year 1

KITTENS

Baby cats are called kittens. For the first few weeks of their lives, kittens sleep most of the time – just like human babies. Although they have eyes and ears when they are born, they cannot hear or see. They drink their mother's milk, and she keeps them safe and warm.

These kittens are three weeks old. Although they can see and hear, they stay very close to the mother cat.

When they are about 10 days old, kittens open their eyes for the first time.

By the time they are three weeks old, they will start moving around. Kittens love to play!

When they are five weeks old, they start eating food. Soon they no longer need to drink milk from their mothers. It is time for the kittens to go to their new home.

At 8 weeks, this young kitten is ready to leave its mother.

Text © 2007, David Waugh; photos: top © Mehmet Sensoy, centre © Armin Hanisch, bottom © Sanja Gjenero

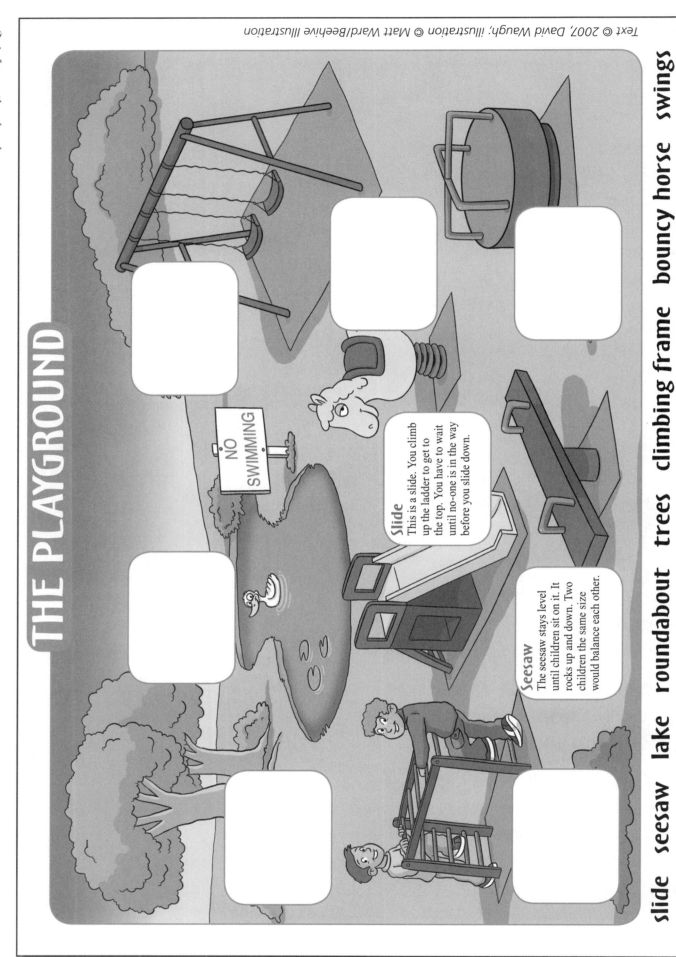

THE PLAYGROUND

Text © 2007, David Waugh; illustration © Matt Ward/Beehive Illustration

NO SWIMMING

Slide
This is a slide. You climb up the ladder to get to the top. You have to wait until no-one is in the way before you slide down.

Seesaw
The seesaw stays level until children sit on it. It rocks up and down. Two children the same size would balance each other.

slide   seesaw   lake   roundabout   trees   climbing frame   bouncy horse   swings

50 Shared texts Non-fiction ● Year 1

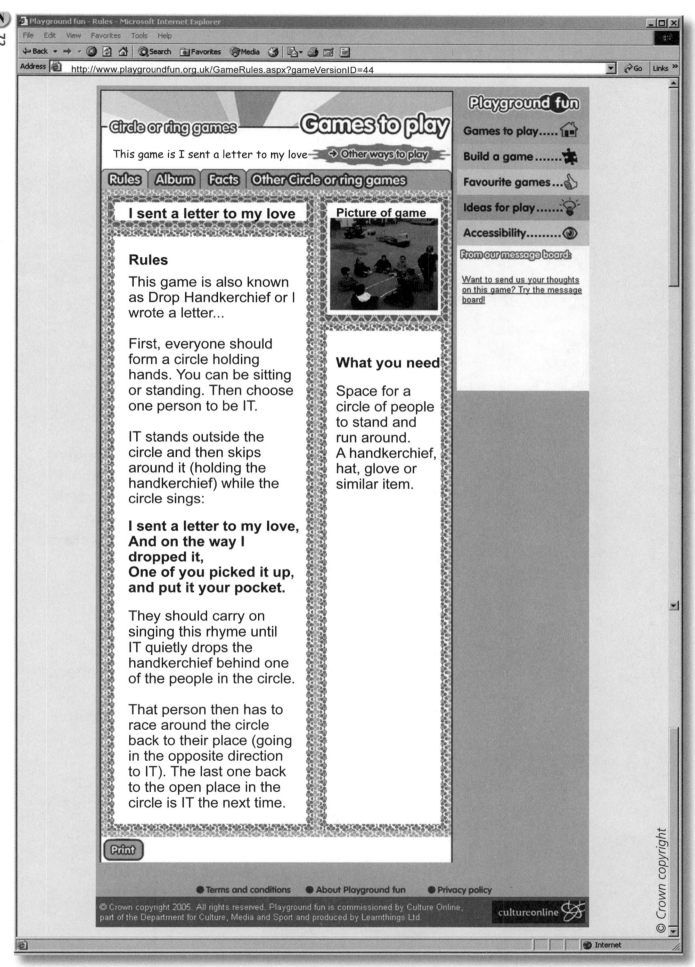

Playground fun - Rules - Microsoft Internet Explorer

File   Edit   View   Favorites   Tools   Help

Back   •   →   •   Search   Favorites   Media

Address   http://www.playgroundfun.org.uk/GameRules.aspx?gameVersionID=44   Go   Links »

Circle or ring games — Games to play

This game is I sent a letter to my love —→ Other ways to play

Rules | **Album** | **Facts** | **Other Circle or ring games**

I sent a letter to my love

Picture of game

Rules

This game is also known as Drop Handkerchief or I wrote a letter...

First, everyone should form a circle holding hands. You can be sitting or standing. Then choose one person to be IT.

IT stands outside the circle and then skips around it (holding the handkerchief) while the circle sings:

I sent a letter to my love, And on the way I dropped it, One of you picked it up, and put it your pocket.

They should carry on singing this rhyme until IT quietly drops the handkerchief behind one of the people in the circle.

That person then has to race around the circle back to their place (going in the opposite direction to IT). The last one back to the open place in the circle is IT the next time.

What you need

Space for a circle of people to stand and run around. A handkerchief, hat, glove or similar item.

Print

Playground fun

Games to play......
Build a game.......
Favourite games...
Ideas for play.......
Accessibility.........

From our message board

Want to send us your thoughts on this game? Try the message board!

● Terms and conditions   ● About Playground fun   ● Privacy policy

© Crown copyright 2005. All rights reserved. Playground fun is commissioned by Culture Online, part of the Department for Culture, Media and Sport and produced by Learnthings Ltd.

cultureonline

Internet

Looking After Animals

What you need to know

Having a pet can be quite a big commitment. You need to be sure that you will be able to look after it properly and make sure that it gets all the attention that it needs.

What you can do

- Be sure that you have enough time and energy to look after your pet.

- Make sure you know someone who will be able to look after your pet if you go on holiday.

- Find out how expensive having a pet will be. You will need to be able to buy all their food, bedding, pet accessories and insurance.

- Make sure that you buy your pet from a reputable dealer, pet shop or animal shelter.

- Register your pet with the local vet.

- Get a reference book about your new pet as this will give you lots of useful information about how to care for and look after them properly.

Text extract from http://www.connexions-direct.com © 2005, Crown copyright. Crown copyright material is reproduced with the permission of the Controller of HMSO and the Queen's printer for Scotland; photos: cat © TOMCRAFT. doa © Maciek Pelc, hamster © Jarek Luczak

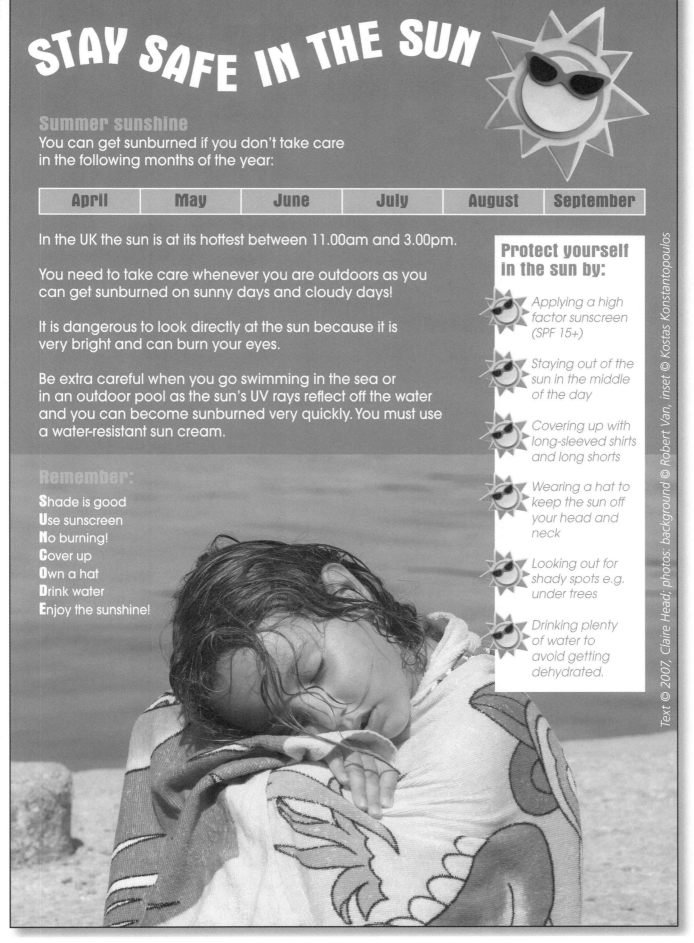

STAY SAFE IN THE SUN

Summer sunshine

You can get sunburned if you don't take care in the following months of the year:

April	May	June	July	August	September

In the UK the sun is at its hottest between 11.00am and 3.00pm.

You need to take care whenever you are outdoors as you can get sunburned on sunny days and cloudy days!

It is dangerous to look directly at the sun because it is very bright and can burn your eyes.

Be extra careful when you go swimming in the sea or in an outdoor pool as the sun's UV rays reflect off the water and you can become sunburned very quickly. You must use a water-resistant sun cream.

Remember:

Shade is good
Use sunscreen
No burning!
Cover up
Own a hat
Drink water
Enjoy the sunshine!

Protect yourself in the sun by:

- Applying a high factor sunscreen (SPF 15+)
- Staying out of the sun in the middle of the day
- Covering up with long-sleeved shirts and long shorts
- Wearing a hat to keep the sun off your head and neck
- Looking out for shady spots e.g. under trees
- Drinking plenty of water to avoid getting dehydrated.

Text © 2007, Claire Head; photos: background © Robert Van, inset © Kostas Konstantopoulos

Make a Telephone

1 Find two disposable plastic cups.
2 Poke a very small hole in the bottom of each with a sharp pencil.
3 Feed string through the holes in each cup.
4 Tie a knot at each end of the string and pull the cups to check they don't come off.
5 Decorate both cups using coloured pens.
6 Work with a partner, and pull the cups taut.
7 Put a cup to your ear and ask your partner to talk into theirs.
8 Can you hear what your partner is saying?

How It Works

The string carries sounds as tiny vibrations, which you can feel if you touch the string. The cup allows your ear to hear these vibrations as sounds.

Text © 2007, Scholastic Ltd; photos © 2006, Jupiter Images Corporation

Why parks attract wildlife

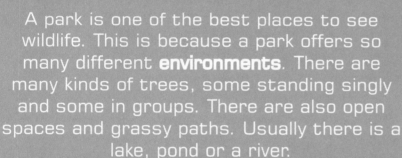

A park is one of the best places to see wildlife. This is because a park offers so many different **environments**. There are many kinds of trees, some standing singly and some in groups. There are also open spaces and grassy paths. Usually there is a lake, pond or a river.

Birds and animals often search for food in open country, but when they are not feeding they hide in trees or bushes, where they can watch what is happening around them. Nearly all wild creatures need to have water for drinking and bathing.

In the countryside, there will be more wild creatures in places which are like parks than in dense woods or open fields. But in the park you will be able to see them more easily, because they become used to people and so are often quite tame.

Text extract from "Use your eyes: in the Park" by Ralph Whitlock © 1986, Ralph Whitlock (1986, Wayland (Publishers) Limited); photos: park © Marthy Marag, squirrel © Mister Eels, duck © Cathy Kaplan, children © Hortongrou, swan © Derek Z

House Sparrows

House sparrows are among the birds we can see almost anywhere in the country. They eat seeds and food which people have put out for them. They build nests near to houses under roofs and next to drainpipes. The mother sparrow lays her eggs and then keeps them warm by sitting on them. Two weeks after the eggs are laid the baby sparrows hatch out of them.

wing

eye

Text © 2007, David Waugh; photos: background © Deborah Frans, inset © Luis Rock

GARDEN BIRDS

SWALLOWS

Swallows catch insects as they are flying. Swallows have long tails. Often we see martins too, but they have shorter tails. Swallows and martins fly to warmer countries for the winter but return in the summer.

BLUE TITS

Blue tits often make nests in gardens. They like to feed on nuts which people hang up in nets. Some people put up bird boxes for blue tits to nest in.

SONG THRUSHES

Thrushes dig for worms and also look for snails to eat. They break the snails' shells by bashing them on a stone and then eat the snail inside. They have speckled chests.

BLACKBIRDS

Blackbirds dig for worms with their beaks. The males sing so that they can attract females. They also sing to tell other male blackbirds to keep away.

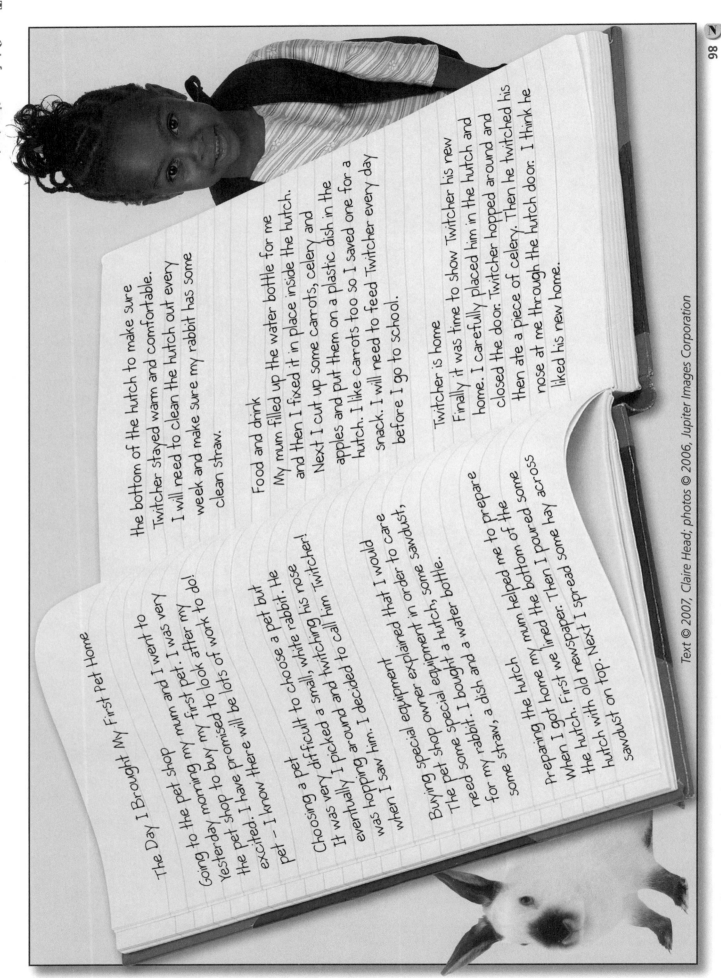

Text © 2007, Claire Head; photos © 2006, Jupiter Images Corporation

WHO COOKS MY SCHOOL DINNER?

My name is Mrs Patrick and I am the cook at Fairhaven Primary School. With the help of a team of people, I cook lunch for one hundred children every school day. There is a lot to do! Here is my busy schedule:

First, I wash my hands and put on my apron and hat. Next, I make a cup of tea. I talk with my team about the menu for the day. We make a list of the food we need.

Then we prepare the food. We follow the recipe carefully to make sure we have enough food for everyone. We try to choose healthy meals.

Now we turn the huge ovens on and start cooking. When lunch is almost ready we set the tables in the school dinner hall. We put a water jug and some cups on each table.

At midday we begin serving lunch to the children. They collect their own plates and cutlery. Everyone is hungry and some people want a second helping.

After lunch we clear up. It takes a long time to wash up and clean the kitchen ready for the next day. When we have finished I am usually ready for another cup of tea!

Text © 2007, Claire Head; photos: notepad © Davide Guglielmo, clock © Sanja Gjenero, cook © 2006, Jupiter Images Corporation

PDSA I for pets in need of vets - Microsoft Internet Explorer

File   Edit   View   Favorites   Tools   Help

← Back   →   ⊗   ▣   ⌂   Search   Favorites   ◆   ▤▾   ▤   ▥   ▾   ▤

Address http://secure.pdsa.org.uk/youngpdsa/reggie_4.php   Go   Links

Diary of a PDSA vet

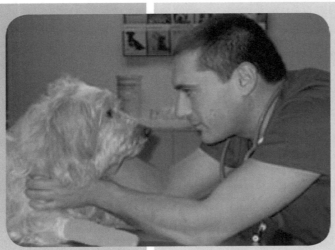

Steve Howard, Senior Veterinary Surgeon at the Swansea PDSA PetAid hospital describes a working day.

Morning

I set off a bit early today, as I've got quite a bit to do at the PetAid hospital. I've also bought myself a new bicycle, which I'm dying to try out! Dressed in all of the safety gear I start off towards the hospital.

As I cycle through the park, I see a lady who is very upset. She's been out with her dog, throwing sticks and one has got stuck in her dog's throat. The dog is obviously in a lot of pain, so without a second to wait, I tell the lady to 'follow me'. The Swansea PDSA PetAid hospital is fortunately only a minute away and I call through on my mobile phone to warn them what is happening. We arrive quickly and I'm greeted by one of the nurses. We rush the dog through to the preparation room and open the dog's mouth. Fortunately the stick has just jammed in the dog's back teeth, so we carefully remove it with a pair of forceps. Sometimes the stick goes all the way down a dog's throat, which can be horrible!

I give the dog an injection of antibiotics, to prevent any infection and the dog is then back to its old self, jumps down off the table and we take him out to his grateful owner.

The receptionist has taken down a few details whilst she was waiting so we now know that the dog is called Duggie. He's a little Jack Russell Terrier with quite a lot of spirit and it's nice to see him running around, even if he is making a lot of noise!

Internet

Illustrations © Simon Rumble/Beehive Illustration

Kylie's Life: Here is a timeline of Kylie's first six years.

Kylie was 4 when she started school in September 2004.

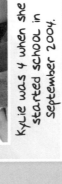

In January 2002 Kylie started going to nursery school.

5 months old. Kylie's first tooth came through.

6 June 2006: Kylie is 6 years old. She is in Y1.

Kylie stopped wearing nappies. She was 3 years old

At 13 months, Kylie started to walk. She also said her first word.

Kylie Walker
b. 23 September 1999

📖 SCHOLASTIC Photocopiable   50 Shared texts Non-fiction ● Year 1

MAKING TOAST

We took a slice of bread out of
the packet.

We put the bread into the toaster.

We set the toaster to the right
number. The higher the number,
the darker your toast is.

While the bread was toasting, we
got out a plate, a knife and some
butter to spread on the toast.

When the toast popped up, we
left it for a short time so that it
didn't burn our fingers.

We spread some butter on the toast –
and then we ate it!

Text © 2007, David Waugh

A SCHOOL TRIP TO THE SEASIDE

Our trip to the seaside began at 9 o 'clock on Monday morning when we set off from the school by bus. We were not allowed to eat on the coach, but the teachers said we could sing.

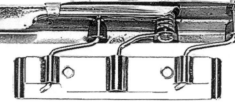

When we reached the seaside we could see the cliffs from the coach. The waves were crashing. There were seagulls everywhere and they were very noisy.

The coach parked and we walked to the beach. We could see the bright lights of the amusement arcades. At the fair there was a big wheel.

On the beach we found shells and stones. We paddled in the sea and ate our picnic.

In the afternoon we looked in rock pools. We found lots of tiny creatures.

Finally, the coach driver brought the coach back and we set off home.

Text © 2007, David Waugh; photos: clipboard © 2006, Jupiter Images Corporation, blue coach (top right) © Bjarne Kvaale, cliffs © Tiago Pontes, big wheel © Martin Walls, girl on beach © Luc Sesselle, seaweed © Kevin Mark Wood, yellow coach (bottom left) © Ben Oates

SCHOLASTIC **Photocopiable**

50 Shared texts Non-fiction ● Year 1

KWL Grid: OWLS

Hi, my name is Sally. I am in class 1B. My class have just finished a project about owls. We have learned a lot. Here is our KWL grid. It took us three weeks to research the information. The 'How' column in the grid below shows you what we did to learn about owls.

Now we are all owl experts!

Know (What do we think we know about owls?)	What (What do I want to find out about owls?)	How (What did we do to find out the information?)	Learned (What have we learned about owls?)
Owls are birds.	What type of bird?	Looked up 'owl' in a dictionary.	Owls are birds of prey.
Owls come out at night.	Why don't we see owls in the daytime?	Used an information book.	Owls are nocturnal. They hunt at night.
They make a 'too-whit-to-whoo' sound.	Why do owls say 'too-whit-to-whoo'?	Researched on the internet.	They make this sound to call each other.
They eat mice, voles, hedgehogs, grass snakes, young birds, fish, insects, bats, rats and frogs.	How do owls catch their prey?	A speaker from an owl sanctuary told us.	Owls have excellent hearing. They can hear animals moving around. They catch their prey in their sharp talons.

Are you as wise as an owl?

OWLS

Text © 2007, Claire Head; photos: top © Eszter Szollosi, bottom left © Juha Blomberg, bottom right © Pamela Menn

GLOSSARY

Birds of prey
birds that hunt other living things for food

Habitat
where a creature lives – its home

Nocturnal
animals that come out at night and sleep in the daytime

Talons
sharp claws

Owls are birds of prey. There are over 170 different species of owls including Barn Owls, Snowy Owls and Tawny Owls.

Owls have round heads, forward-facing eyes and small, pointed beaks. Most owls have soft brown, grey or white feathers.

Owls can be found in every part of the world except in Antarctica. Most owls prefer to live in a woodland habitat.

Owls are mainly nocturnal. They hunt at night using their excellent hearing and eyesight. Owls eat mice, grass snakes, frogs, fish and young birds. They swoop down silently and seize their prey in their sharp talons.

Owls often make a screeching noise. Sometimes you can hear owls calling 'too-whit-to-whoo' to each other.

■ SCHOLASTIC **Photocopiable**

50 Shared texts Non-fiction ● Year 1

Wrapping it up

Manufacturers, the people who make things, package most food before it goes to the shops. They put it in boxes and cartons, bags and cans, jars and bottles. Some packaging is made of plastic, some of glass, and some of paper and cardboard.

What is packaging for?

● Packaging helps to protect food and keep it fresh.

● Packaging makes food easy to store in the shops and easy to take home.

● Packaging helps customers to see what they are buying. It gives them information about what is inside.

● Food is packaged in different sizes, so customers can buy the amount they need.

Designers plan how to package food in the best way.

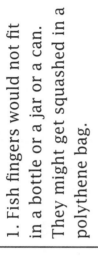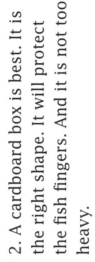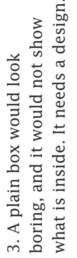

1. Fish fingers would not fit in a bottle or a jar or a can. They might get squashed in a polythene bag.

2. A cardboard box is best. It is the right shape. It will protect the fish fingers. And it is not too heavy.

3. A plain box would look boring, and it would not show what is inside. It needs a design.

Most of the things we buy have packaging for the same reasons.

Text extract and illustrations from "How things are made" by Steve Parker © 1992, Kingfisher Publications plc

✑ What is a bike made of?

A bicycle has hundreds of parts, made of all sorts of materials.

The **saddle** is made of plastic, with foam padding for comfort and a vinyl cover.

The parts come from factories in several countries around the world.

frame
a metal called chromoly – a type of steel

handlebar grip
rubber

brake lever
steel

brake cable
steel covered in nylon

fork
chromoly

hub
aluminium

spoke
steel

wheel rim
aluminium

chain
steel

valve
steel and brass

brake caliper
aluminium

valve cap
plastic

tyre
rubber

Text extract and illustrations from "How things are made" by Steve Parker © 1992, Kingfisher Publications plc

Thursday, 17 June

15 Calicut Road
Badagara
Kerala
India

Dear Tom,

Thank you for your letter. I enjoyed reading about what you do at school. My school is near to my house so it takes me ten minutes to walk there. Do you walk to school every day?

This is what happened at my school today:

My favourite lesson is Geography because we learn about different countries. What's your favourite lesson at school? At play time I like to play football with my friends. What do you play?

From

Sunil

My timetable	Thursday
8.00-8.40	Assembly
8.40-9.15	Hindi
9.15-9.30	Play time
9.30-10.30	English
10.30-11.30	Maths
11.30-12.30	Lunch
12.30-1.00	Geography
1.00-1.30	Malayalam
1.30-1.45	Play time
1.45-2.15	Games
2.15-2.45	Singing

Acknowledgements

The publishers gratefully acknowledge permission to reproduce the following copyright material:

Aladdin Books Ltd for the use of an extract 'Leaves' from *Plants (Fascinating Science Series)* by Sally Hewitt © 2001, Aladdin Books Ltd (2001, Franklin Watts) and an extract and illustrations 'Light for life' from *Science for Fun: Light and Colour* by Gary Gibson © 1994, Aladdin Books Ltd (1994, Watts Books). **Anita Ganeri** for the use of an extract 'How do we move?' from *Find out about the body* by Anita Ganeri © 1994, Anita Ganeri/BBC Education (1994, BBC Education). **Her Majesty's Stationery Office** for the use of an extract 'Games to play: Circle or ring games' and the website page from http://www.playgroundfun.org.uk © Crown copyright. **Her Majesty's Stationery Office** for the use of an extract 'Looking after animals' from www.connexions-direct.com © 2005, Crown copyright material is reproduced with the permission of the Controller of HMSO and the Queen's Printer for Scotland. **Hodder and Stoughton Ltd** for the use of an extract and illustrations from *The Senses – Touch* edited by Mandy Suhr © 1993, Wayland (Publishers) Ltd (1993, Wayland (Publishers) Ltd. **Kingfisher Publications Plc** for the use of text extracts 'Wrapping it up' and 'What is a bike made of?' and illustrations from *How things are made* by Steve Parker © 1992, Kingfisher Publications Plc. **Oxford University Press** for the use of an extract 'Waste' from *Exploring where you live* by Terry Jennings © 1995, Terry Jennings (1995, Oxford Reading Tree). **PDSA**, the Veterinary Charity, for the use of an extract from 'Diary of a Vet' by Steve Howard from the PDSA website www.pdsa.org.uk/youngpdsa © 2006, PDSA (2006, www.pdsa.org.uk). **Scholastic Children's Books** for the use of the back cover of *The A–Z of ghosts, skeletons and other haunting horrors* by Tracey Turner, illustrated by Kate Sheppard cover © 2004, Scholastic Children's Books (2004, Scholastic Children's Books). **Watts Publishing Group** for the use of the index from *Get Set Go! Vegetables* by Judy Bastyra © 1994, Judy Bastyra (1994, Franklin Watts) and for the use of an extract 'Why Parks attract wildlife' from *Use your eyes: In the park* by Ralph Whitlock © 1986, Ralph Whitlock (1986, Wayland (Publishers) Ltd).

Every effort has been made to trace copyright holders for the works reproduced in this book, and the publishers apologise for any inadvertent omissions.